OCEANS

C000003472

CONT.

Oceans Seven

How I cheated death and broke
the hardest record in swimming

ATTILA MÁNYOKI
with Martin Schauhuber

For Mom,
who was always there for me

OCEANS SEVEN

FOREWORD

What you are about to read is not a sugarcoated, cleaned-up version of my life, but the raw thoughts and feelings that I went through as I experienced the events described in this book. They may not always seem reasonable and I may come off as rude at times, but patience can be hard to find after hours of swimming in choppy water. My apologies to everybody who took offence at that.

Marathon swimming can seem like a very lonely sport at times, but I couldn't have done this without the help and support of many people, some of which you will get to know in this book: my family, the pilots and organizers who make this sport possible, my friends who sacrificed vacation time and fought seasickness to accompany me on swims, all the amazing swimmers I got to train with, from fellow Oceans Seven athletes to the folks at all the various lovely recreational swimming groups. No matter how fast you are, I respect you. Our community truly is one of a kind.

I want to thank everyone who has supported or followed me throughout the years. I want to particularly recognize the following people whose support has been instrumental in my journey, who hugely contributed to who I am and what I have achieved. Who enable me to do what I love, to live my life according to and follow my passion and dreams.

Monika Pais and our family. Akos Reinhardt, Andras Takacs and his family, Andras Nagy, Antal Bobics, Aris Polizos, Arpad Kincses, Attila Kocsi, Attila Palkovits, Attila and Krisztina Madaras, Balazs Strobl, Balazs Veszpremi,

Csaba Agh, Csaba Nemeth, Csaba Puskas, Csaba Rozinay, Csaba Toth, Cameron Bellamy, Bill Goding, Dan Simonelli, Darren Miller, Dezso Dobor, Dimitris Kakaklikas, Dr. Antal Szabo, Dr. Bob Darling and the Ulster Hospital, Dr. Zsuzsa Csisztu, Dr. Norbert Ketskes, Dr. Zsolt Sule, Dr. Peter Duska, Dr. Peter Szasz, Dr. Laszlo Tulipan, Dr. Istvan Takacs, Dr. Tunde Fischer, Elina Athanasiadi Siafaris, Elizabeth Fry, Erika and Jeno Kaszas, Ervin Dittrich, Ferenc Elekes, Gabor Tompa, Gary Knox, Giannis Kotsiopoulos, Gyorgy Kovacs, Gyorgy Lendvai, Gyorgy Pal, Hannes Fuchs, Ion Lazarenco Tiron, Istvan Szanati, Jacqueline McClelland, Janney and Bill Murtha, Janos Gyore and his family, Janos Mate, Jeff Kozlovich, Jose Luis Larrosa, Kinga Mathe, Krisztina Pados, Lajos Bokany, Laszlo Dorman, Laszlo Filo, Laszlo Halmos, Laszlo Szanto, Laura Gutierrez Diaz, Masayuki Moriya, Martin Strain and the Chunky Dunkers, Matthias Kaßner, Michael P. Read, Miklos Barabas, Milo McCourt, Ned Denison and the Sandycove swimmers, Nikitas Chouchoutas, Nikos Gemelos and the Olympiacos Swimming Team, Padraig Mallon and the entire Infinity Team, Panos Pontidas, Peter Gyaraki, Philip Rush, Richard Szentes, Roland Bodoki, Sandor Szabo, Sandor Toth, Steven Minaglia, Steven Munatones, Steve Walker, Szabolcs Horvath and the ZKSE Team, Tamas and Krisztina Den, Tunde Szabo, the communities and mayors of Zalaegerszeg, Zoltan Nagy, Zoltan Konya, Zsolt Hadri, Zsuzsa Ban, Yuko Matsuzaki,

and you, Martin.

PROLOGUE

April 2017, New Zealand

"Sorry guys, but that's it. The season is over," Philip says.

The world turns black. I feel like an invisible boxer just punched me in the gut.

"You can come back next year," he says.

Up until this point, I've spent five weeks here on the southern tip of New Zealand's North Island. To others, the island is beautiful. To me, it's the godforsaken end of the world – and maybe the end of my career. I'm supposed to cross the Cook Strait between the North and South Island. If I can't swim, my sponsors may stop supporting me. They're okay with me almost drowning. They're not okay with me not trying.

"I'm not sure if I can come back," I tell Philip.

Back in my room, I collapse into a corner and stare at the wall.

Late at night, Philip calls me. I get my chance.

The next morning, we're on the boat to our starting point on the South Island. One of the old skippers is grumpy. "On days like this, we usually don't go out," he says as we leave.

I should have a two-hour timeframe if the conditions on the coast are okay. Not perfect, not even good, but okay. That will have to be enough. By the time the weather turns bad, I'll be out on the open water. Philip promised me: If I want to swim, he will let me.

On the outside, I play the professional, but inside, I am

screaming out in joy.

The waves toss our boat around like a little toy.

"I never get nauseous on ships," I think to myself as I hang onto the boat's railing, throwing up into the choppy water.

Once we get to the starting point, Philip looks at me. "So…?"

The sea looks much worse than I hoped. But I flew across the globe. I waited for weeks. I struggled through this boat ride. "I will try," I say. One of the old skippers puts his hands on my shoulders and stares into my eyes. "You are a brave man," he says. I'm not sure if he approves of my decision.

Philip gets himself ready. The main boat is too big to stay close to me when I swim, so he lowers his orange rubber dinghy into the water and jumps in.

No matter how much protective cream I put on my skin before jumping in, there's always this breathtaking shock when I jump into the freezing water. A jolt of electricity goes through my body, piercing my core and getting stuck there. For a while, it feels as there's this tension that expands throughout my belly and chest, until I fight it off and get my body moving.

The waves have pushed the ship back, so we are closer to the shore than we planned. I need to start off strongly to avoid the rocks and there are far more jellyfish than expected, but they usually hover at around a meter below the surface. As I swim above them, I see their transparent domes, waiting for me to make a careless move. A leg or an arm reaching down too far as I move through the water. Sure, I know jellyfish are not evil creatures plotting to hurt me. But swimming face-first into a Portuguese man o' war will leave you with some hard feelings towards them.

Most swimmers give up at a wind speed of around 15 to 20 knots – about 37 kilometers per hour. I *start* at 20 knots. "It will get worse after around two hours," Philip told me on the boat as the waves threw themselves against its hull.

In the water, it sort of feels like I am stuck inside a washing machine. I'm the dirty laundry that gets tossed around jagged rocks and venomous jellyfish.

The freezing slaps of the waves pull me away from the worries of the last five weeks and throw me into reality. I'm a boxer hearing the final notes of his entrance song. This is when it matters.

This is my big fight.

I find my rhythm and make my way through the dangerous, rocky start.

Hours pass.

Long-distance swimming can get monotonous, but this monotony sometimes makes way for some magical things. A few hours after the start, a pod of cheerful dolphins joins me. To swim with them reminds one of how easy swimming is. How fast and effortlessly a living creature can move through water relieves me.

It's just water.

The waves have mostly faded by now. Swim. The dolphins jump out of the water and, in a perfect arch, back into the water. Swim.

I still haven't seen a shark. I prefer it this way.

Every twenty minutes, it is feeding time. That word may sound weird, but it's fitting. Philip hands me my drinks and gels, I wolf them down as quickly as possible and then: swim. Philip is always perfectly on time. Hours of training in the pool at home have tuned my inner clock quite well, but I still rely on the feeding as my backup stopwatch. It's easy to lose track of time after four hours in the open water. Eat, swim, swim, swim, eat, swim, swim, swim, eat.

Five or six hours must have passed. I can see the finishing line: barren, rocky hills with a few sorry bushes. They could not look more beautiful to me. I must be around two kilometers from the coast, a little more than thirty minutes of swimming at my usual pace.

I'm still feeling strong. My arms pierce the surface of the water like I mean it. Splash, pull, shoulder up, arm out, arm forward, splash. You can tell that you are losing power when the arms merely fall into the water, happily succumbing to gravity. I won't let this happen. This is why I trained with a snorkel for months: less oxygen, more stamina.

The dolphins have left me a while ago. Philip waves me over: feeding time.

Swim.

I'm not getting any closer to the coastline. The hills must still be about 1.5 kilometers away.

Something must be wrong.

I'm not moving forward. The current is too strong. For every meter my arms pull me ahead, the tide drags me back two with a relentless grip.

Futility tires the mind, and when the mind weakens, so does the body.

Swim. Stronger. Faster. Next feeding. I'm not moving.

Philip changes the boat's course to lead me onto a turn to the left. I'm now swimming parallel to the coastline, catching glimpses of those boring hills every time I turn my head to the right to breathe. I don't know what this means, but I know I must trust my pilot. When I am in the water, he is the boss. Him saying "come back next year" seems like it was a long time ago. I know I can trust him; he wants my success as much as I do. And he has the data. I only have my swim trunks, my goggles and the ocean.

Feed. Swim.

I should have touched the rocks on the North Island an hour ago.

The sea is winning. I don't know if I can make it and that thought is the first step towards defeat.

I am moving my arms, but I'm not making any headway. It's like wanting to run away from something in a nightmare, but no matter what I do, the monster chasing me comes closer and closer.

We are turning towards the shore again.

I must have swum three or four kilometers along the coastline, I can now feel that the tide is weaker. I can progress: splash, pull, shoulder up, arm out, splash. Second wind, they call it. Splash, splash, splash.

I see the hills coming closer. New Zealand's North Island, its beauty almost as renowned as the South Island's, is reaching out to me, extending a delicate hand. I just need to grab it.

If only I could see what's in the water.

This hand I'm about to grab has jagged nails. In order to finish, I must touch the rocky coast, but there is a myriad of rocks and crags with razor-sharp edges in the water before it. As if the jellyfish from the start had turned to stone, now hunting for blood instead of mere pain.

I must swim slowly, controlled.

Some last, exhausted splashes. I reach out.

Finish.

A wave catches me from behind.

I'm being carried towards the rock, but my exhausted arms manage to save me. I push myself off.

I have won the battle.

There's a messy storm of emotions inside me. The feeling is only there for a few seconds before the pain comes, but these few seconds are unbelievable. Nothing can match its intensity.

This is what I live for. Life is about being happy. I find happiness in this.

A giant wave crashes into me, but I'm far enough from the rocks not to get hurt.

I hear shouts from the boat. I know Philip is glad that he trusted me.

I think about Móni and the girls. How proud they will be. I climb onto the boat and scream of joy.

My career is saved. I will be able to go back to Northern Ireland to face the only swim that has ever defeated me: the frozen hell that is the North Channel.

SWIMMING THE WORLD CUP

September 1991, Greece

Ever since I swam in Lake Balaton for the first time, I knew where I belonged. It's been more than two years since then, I've just celebrated my 18th birthday – and I know what I want to do with my life. There is enough money in open water competitions that I may be able to make a career out of it.

I fly to Koroni on the Greek peninsula of Peloponnese. Ruins of some old castle here, a restaurant offering amazing fish there, a church christened to St. Nicholas, and, best of all, no tourists outside of holiday season. Your average Greek village. And one of the most important places of my young life: Here, I will swim my first international competition.

Days before the swim, I am having lunch with a Bulgarian coach when a hornet flies up to my face. Before I can do anything, it stings me just underneath my right eye.

I'm allergic to hornets.

I barely notice the pain because I am panicking about how fast the sting swells up. The coach puts a cloth with some chemicals on where the hornet stung me.

It burns. Horribly. My skin looks like it turns to liquid.

Soon after, the swelling stops. But the area below my eye stays so puffy that I can't fully open my eye. The coach wraps a big bandage over my face, but I have doubts whether I will be able to put on my swim goggles.

Race day comes, and fortunately, my face feels healthy enough for me to get in the water. Almost 35 kilometers, the longest race I have ever swum.

I feel great during the race. I do have to stop to fix my goggles more often than usual, but it's not as bad as I feared.

I'm fast. Fast enough to come in second in my first international race!

Eight hours and three minutes. I will never forget this time. Now, I really know where I belong.

Open water is so much more enjoyable than pool lanes. I enjoy the parties, the merciless competition in the water and the unique sense of camaraderie outside of it. At every event, I meet dozens of new people, many of them eventually becoming my friends.

I live a young man's dream life. Every week is a whirlwind of people, parties, and fun. I swim well enough in some of the competitions to earn my first invite to a top-level swim: the 1993 German Open in Fürth. Even the biggest stars from the World Cup are here.

We swim 30 kilometers in a channel. I have zero experience with races like this, so when the whole group squeezes together as we swim around a buoy, I get kicked in my right shoulder. Minute by minute, my mobility wears down and is replaced by a growing pain. At around the 20-kilometers mark, I decide to give up. I cannot risk my health a week before my biggest race yet.

And that would be nothing less than the World Cup final in Italy.

There, the top 35 swimmers from the World Cup and a few lucky so-called Green Card invitees swim a 42-kilometer race. The competition takes place in the aptly named village Finale Ligure, a bit more than halfway from Nice to Genoa. It is one of those places that make you remember how blessed you are to do this for a living: an unpretentious haven, made to enjoy life. Yes, there are some touristy apartment blocks and the highway runs between the villages and the sea. But I grew up close to Lake Balaton – I was never one to judge a place for being accessible for the masses.

In Finale Ligure, a long beach leads towards a magnificent cliff. The locals call it Caprazoppa, tourists call it "Let's take a photo!"

I call it my office for a weekend.

There is no chance in hell that I finish anywhere near the top ten, but I don't mind. Swimming at this level will be enough to keep me in this circus for a long time.

After my first international swim in 1991 (2nd from the right)

1996

I have heard stories about Argentina, but those can't do reality justice. In the days before the competition, there is a palpable feeling of excitement in the air. Once race day arrives, I understand what people were talking about.

We start in Santa Fe and swim down to Coronda. 57 kilometers sounds impossible, but the river carries us downstream. Spectators in boats line the river and party up above on the bridges. It's a carnival. "Almost a hundred thousand people," another swimmer tells me after the race.

Next, Rio Parana awaits me. When I heard of this 88-kilometer race for the first time, I genuinely thought I was being pranked. But again: downstream. The fastest guys finish in less than ten hours.

I did not expect to win races in my first seasons, but the competition is brutal. On a good day, I can keep up with the faster guys for a little while. I feel like they should be breaking down with me swimming away from them, smiling and waving. But it is the other way around. Just without the smiles and waves.

When I realize that I am falling back, I get even more exhausted. And then, giving up ends up being my only option.

A few hours after the swim, I feel deflated. I remember how good I felt in training and I feel like I could have done better. But there's always the next race. Maybe this time, I'll finish strong.

Mar del Plata. Lake Memphremagog. Lac Saint-Jean. Atlantic City. Ohrid. The Nile. The! Nile! The Suez Canal. Sharm el Sheikh.

The little kid from Zalaegerszeg is travelling the world.

In the off-season, the little kid from Zalaegerszeg hangs out in Budapest. Bike tours, long nights with friends, some training.

And then it's on again: Argentina, Canada, the United States, Egypt, Macedonia, Germany, about 15 or 16 events a year. It's not just World Cup competitions: The prize money in Egypt is good enough to make some of the good swimmers come anyway.

All those races have little meaning to me. I finish, get out of the water and get on with my life. Onto the next plane, on to the next place, on to the next party. Sure, I train hard. But when I get close to my limit, I don't mind quitting.

I underestimated the role luck plays in our sport. Sometimes, the conditions change during the race and my plan falls apart. It's tough when you were planning for nine hours of still water, but some winds off the Eastern Canadian shore start messing with you two hours after the start.

In Mar del Plata, I get a taste of what I could achieve when things go my way. From the start of the race, I feel powerful, and when I hit the finish line, I feel like I could've pushed far more. Whatever. 12th place is my best result yet in my nascent career.

Happily, I get ready to leave for the next race.

I love this.

2003

I hate this.

The World Cup was more fun ten years ago. Most of the other swimmers and coaches agree with me.

Saturday, I swim in Lamia, Greece. On Sunday afternoon, they drive me to the airport. I fly from Athens to Budapest, drive home, swap out my bags and go back to the airport. Budapest to Zürich, Zürich to New York, New York to Montreal, Montreal to Quebec City, Quebec City to St. John. I arrive on Wednesday. That same evening, the formal part of the competition starts. Presentations, press conferences, sponsors. On Saturday, we swim the competition.

Sunday, it's on to the US.

That 12th place at Mar del Plata in 1996 is still my best result. My ranking does not improve, but the prize money is good enough to live off it. I'm not enjoying this lifestyle anymore, but as long as I can make a living by swimming, I have to keep going. It's not like I have a degree to fall back on.

Maybe I'll improve one day.

THE LAST RACE

September 11, 2004, Atlantic City

Nothing is normal here in Atlantic City. Flashing lights, casinos, boardwalk candy. And, fittingly, one of the most unusual swimming competitions. We are swimming in a lagoon, twisting and turning through the landmass that looks like a hand with too many fingers. There are no escort boats or fixed feeding points, so everybody comes up with a different plan on where to meet their coach. Many just ask a local waterfront homeowner for a spot in their garden from which they can throw their swimmer a drink.

I made my decision. This will be my last race in the World Cup series. From now, I will only compete in individual events.

The day before the race is amazing. There is a charity event for kids with Down syndrome where I get to swim 50 meters with one of them, cheering him on like they are in a race. Afterwards, we have our open training session. My good friends Petar Stoychev, Damian Blaum and Gabriel Chailou swim next to me. As we arrive at the finish line, the boats turn on their lights and perform a guard of honor. As we arrive on the deck, everybody is clapping.

I breathe in this whole moment. I inhale the love they show me.

Maybe it all was good for something after all.

The race is on September 11, 2004, the third anniversary of the terrorist attacks on the Twin Towers. That makes it an unusually popular event and that is a problem. There are more swimmers than coaches around, so I have nobody to give me a drink. I'll just try my luck and ask somebody else's coach if I can get a drink.

Whenever there are too many swimmers, it is important to have a good start.

Mine is not one of them.

Instead of wasting my energy trying to pass through this mess of arms and legs in front of me, I stay back and swim with the crowd. I will just win the race later.

Occasionally, somebody falls back, but the larger group stays together for the most part. After about seven kilometers, I try my luck. Full speed, like I was swimming a few pool lengths.

The water is way too warm. Exhausted, I slow down to my normal pace. I check my surroundings.

I passed a grand total of: one guy.

And now, I feel tired.

There is no chance I'll get a good finish.

I see a lady in a garden and swim up to her. "Excuse me, could I get a drink?"

I can tell she was not expecting that. "Oh, uh, sure," she says and walks into the house. She comes back with a glass of water. I'd have preferred something sugary, I thought all people here drink was Coke and Dr. Pepper. But I'm happy either way.

I enjoy my nice, fresh glass of water – it tastes like it came from the bottle, not the tap – and watch the field of swimmers pull away.

Way out of reach.

Who cares?

I put on autopilot and finish the last three kilometers as if I were in slow-motion.

27th.

It is over.

Nobody gives a damn if you're 27th. I swam an alright 10-kilometer race, just had some bad luck with the conditions. It doesn't matter anyways. 27th, 17th or 7th, at home, nobody cares either way. All that matters is football, football, football.

I'm tired. I'm tired of all the swimming, I'm tired of those goddamn airplanes, I'm even more tired of the security check at airports, I'm tired of losing races, I'm tired of the weather messing up my swims, I'm tired of other swimmers getting in my way, I'm tired of not winning for my club and my federation, I'm tired of all the training, I'm tired of currents changing mid-race, I'm tired of waves filling my mouth with water when I try to breathe, I'm tired of my swimming goggles cutting into my face, I'm tired of feeling exhausted when I still have three kilometers to go, I'm tired of the sand at beach swims, I'm tired of the same guys beating me over and over again, I'm tired of always being away from home, I want to cry, I want to cry

I don't want this anymore

It's over.

A NEW LIFE

2005, Greece

"No excuses. You swim."

Nikos speaks with a deep voice. I stare at him.

Six hours ago, I did not know this man. Nikos is my friend Giannis Kotsopoulos' coach, he joined us for the drive from Athens to Thessaloniki. For the past four hours, we have been talking non-stop. He keeps asking painful questions, questions that deserve the truth. So I speak the truth. And so does he.

"It's not the waves, not the other swimmers, not the current."

I freeze and almost speak up.

"It's only you who decides if you succeed," Nikos goes on.

And, in one instant, all those swirling thoughts inside my brain fall to the floor like dead butterflies.

"Only you. No excuses."

It echoes in my head. No excuses.

I feel it: He is right.

He does not move. We can both sense the importance of this moment.

I look at Nikos.

His serious gaze is fixated on me. A little squint tells me that he is surprised.

It must be obvious what his words have done to me.

"No excuses." These words engraved themselves into my brain the second they reached my ears.

"You swim only for yourself, not for anybody else. Not your parents, not your club, not me. You will be the one reaching or not reaching your goals. Not the weather, not other swimmers. No excuses."

No excuses.

It has been a tough few hours since I found out that I was completely wrong. I guess we all think that we know exactly who we are. At least I thought I knew. The beliefs Nikos shattered on that car ride were my very core: I told myself I was great, but unlucky. I had built my life around this illusion. Now that it is gone, I feel like somebody else. I am still Attila, a short Hungarian guy…but, oh, so different. It's the most confused I have ever felt. I was so used to thinking with that tunnel vision every minute of the day, seeing life only one way, thinking only one way, dreaming only one way, swimming only one way, having the same standpoint in discussions. There was only one way. *My* way, the *right* way.

I think this is what everybody is like. But most people are not as wrong as I was about the way I did things.

Now Nikos has grabbed me by the shoulders, pulled me up and turned me around. No more tunnel vision.

I have found a mentor.

"It is time to set a goal, Attila," Nikos says. "A big one."

"I don't know what. I don't know what I can do."

"Dare to dream," he says. I look up. His stare pierces into me. As if he knew that something is there but I am afraid of it myself.

It must be one big swim. Something special. Maybe something that has never been done.

"Think of home, my friend," he says.

He means Lake Balaton. There is no other way, nothing else in Hungary makes sense.

"How?" I ask.

"How long is it?" Nikos asks, his voice rising as he challenges me. It is phrased like a question, but it is a statement: You will swim this.

"About 80 kilometers."

"See! Train hard and you can do it."

Impossible. 80 kilometers is crazy and that's what I tell him.

"It is possible. You believe in yourself, you work hard and then you do it."

I shake my head and let out a desperate laugh.

"Then you will have done it and then you will know that it was *not* impossible," he goes on. "You just don't know your limits."

He is crazy. This is crazy.

"I will think about it," I say.

I call some older friends who have swum 70-kilometer-races.

"No."

"You can't, no."

"No, my friend."

"I don't think so."

I tell Nikos.

"They are not even on your level physically, but they do it," he says. "Because they want it!"

I do not want it for a reason: I know I cannot do it.

"Attila, you can do this. Not tomorrow, but if you work,

then you can."

Swimming across Lake Balaton would be huge. It is almost impossible to get the Hungarian public pay attention to open water swimming, but if there is one way, it is by crossing our national sanctuary.

80 kilometers is too much, though. I don't have the experience.

No excuses, I remember. No excuses.

I breathe in deeply. And out slowly.

"Okay," I say before my inner self can disagree.

Nikos' eyes widen. He nods.

"Yes, Attila. This will be your goal, and you will work hard for it. Remember: No excuses."

I feel the energy flowing through my body, spreading from my heart outwards. Everything is buzzing.

"You will have to change many things, my friend," Nikos says, starting off a monologue. He talks about hardships and preparations, about responsibility, about commitment.

By the end of it, I know my future. A new training system, a new mentality: There is no quitting early. Start, train, finish when it's over. No skipping. Nothing that is not good for me. No more parties.

From now on, I will not try to fit my trainings around the rest of my day. Now the rest of my day will have to fit around the trainings.

No excuses.

ROAD TO BALATON

2005–2007, Greece/Hungary

Over the next two years, I only swim at a few small events to earn some money. Otherwise, my life consists of training. Even when I struggle, I enjoy it. It is tough to work so hard for a goal that may still be years away. But my life finally has meaning. There is a difference between solely waking up and waking up for your dream.

I spend half of the year in Athens, the other half I live in Hungary with my mom. I don't check the results of the swimmers I used to compete against anymore. It's only about me and my training.

Half the battle is keeping my mind focused on the goal. The leaves turn brown, I train, snow falls, I train, spring comes, I train, the summer heat passes, I train, the leaves turn brown again.

I train. I train. I train. I train. I train. I train. Every day but Sundays. 707 days in total.

Every letter on this page is a training day on the way to Balaton.

BALATON

Finally, the day has come. I feel ready.

As I drive down to Lake Balaton, I remember coming here for my first race with Sándor, the lifeguard from the pool at home. In a way, the journey I started then is beginning anew today.

I have never been in a better shape physically – and mentally, I am in a different world now. Three long years I worked for this and now it is finally time to reap the fruits.

80 kilometers is an incomprehensible distance for a swimmer, but I know I will finish, probably in around 24 hours. I have rarely trained in darkness as it's forbidden to swim in lakes after 9 p.m. and all the pools close around that time. Only once, with the help of the lifeguard János, I got a taste of swimming in the dark. "I'm the only one here after all the people leave. I'll let you in," he told me one day. The next day, I arrived at the pool at 10 p.m., snuck in, swam about 25 kilometers in six hours and left before anybody else in Zalaegerszeg even woke up.

As the day of the swim comes closer, more and more thoughts about having to swim in the dark lake creep into my mind – but there is no danger. There are no sharks in Balaton.

Everything is well prepared. The company that provides the boat has taken care of the swimming license. It is bureaucratic hell to get it for this kind of swim because there are so many boats crossing from the northern shore to the southern shore. My friend Attila – yes, it's a common name in Hungary – will take care of my feedings. Dozens of friends are with me, standing at the lake's shores. I am only thinking about the swim. No worries about anything else.

I start in the afternoon at the Hotel Marina Port in Balatonkenese, a small town at the eastern tip of the lake.

For months, I was wondering how I would feel once I was in the water.

Well…it is the same as always. Just as it is in the pool, it is one stroke after the other. Nikos told me not to think too much about the many, many hours of swimming that will follow. It will be a long day anyways.

Swimming is pure joy. All that training finally finds its purpose. One of the truly great things about swimming is how easy it can feel if the body is positioned perfectly.

Balaton is long, but narrow. About a third of the way, the peninsula Tihany extends far into the lake. There, the distance between the northern and southern shores is only about 1.3 kilometers. Tihany is my first mental checkpoint. From the start, I can see it, and once I have passed it, I will have a better idea of my pace. If I reach it after six hours, that's good. If it takes me eight hours, that's still okay.

There's no way it will take me eight hours, though. I am fast. The feedings and hours pass like a breeze. Tihany is getting closer much faster than I expected; even through my goggles, I can already see the pier sticking out on the east side.

But this is a marathon. No point getting excited about a fast split time.

Swim.

The weather is turning for the worse. Old me would have started to complain now. That Attila would be stuck in his head, pitying himself for the bad luck he is having.

No excuses.

Three hours into my 24-hour-masterpiece, they force me to quit. "Get out! Fast! Storm warning!" the pilot tells me.

I want to keep swimming, but that doesn't matter. The boat is made from aluminium and the engine is powered by electricity.

It essentially is a lightning rod.

As I leave the water, I sense a black maw opening inside me. It was all in vain. The license was only valid for a day and the amount of organizing that is necessary makes it impossible to try again this year.

For three long years, I have worked for this dream. Now it is shattered, together with me.

"This will teach you to be much stronger," Nikos says.

He must be kidding. I believed that my coach truly understood me.

Maybe a phone call simply cannot convey how destroyed I am. I can barely make out the rest of our conversation.

What hurts the most is that I didn't get to prove everybody wrong. People have been looking down on me all my life. If you're as short as I am, you know the many ways a human can smile. The genuine smile, the condescending smile, the smile shaped by pity. "Oh, you want to be a good swimmer. How cute," they say.

This was the day when I was supposed to show them. I didn't fail, but I didn't succeed either.

I just didn't get to prove it.

CHILDHOOD MEMORIES:
OPEN WATER

August 1989, Balatonfüred

As Attila approached his 16th birthday, he could hardly imagine a life without swimming. Not metaphorically – he just wouldn't have known what to do otherwise. He'd always enjoyed swimming, but with each passing year, his life revolved around it more and more. Sure, he cared about some other things. But whenever something came up, his first thought was: "How does it fit with my training schedule?"

25 meters, turn, 25 meters, turn. When he talked to friends who didn't swim, they never really understood it. Sure, Hungarians love swimming, but unless you do it every day, you won't understand how the mind is conditioned to think in these 25-meter intervals. At every turn, you can lose a race. Between the turns, you can win it.

One day, it was different. National championships were being held at Lake Balaton. Of course, Attila had swum in this lake before – every Hungarian has – but never like this. He had never tried to be fast, to win a race, to act like it was a pool. In Hungary, they call this sport "hosszútávúszás".

Open water swimming.

The year before, Sándor had taken Attila to watch the race from a boat and escort a swimmer. Afterwards, he had kept saying how he wanted to swim there next year.

Sándor always was a reliable guy.

Attila competed in the 14-kilometer race from Balatonfüred to Siofok, the two largest towns on Lake Balaton. There were no separate starts by age classes, so he had to swim next to 25-year-olds. At the harbor, they jumped in and started swimming. It was a little chaotic in the beginning, but people got in line fast. They were all experts in swimming in overcrowded lanes.

Attila tried to get into a rhythm, but something was different. He didn't need to find a rhythm. He already had it. And with that, a feeling of belonging in this open water. That young swimmer darted across the lake's surface like no one else could. No turns, no breaks, no limits.

"This is what animals raised in a zoo must feel like when they are released into the wild," he thought. Every stroke of the arms and every kick of the legs put a bigger smile in his heart. The movements may have been the same, but they felt different. He was surrounded by pure nature. He didn't have time to look out across the vast lake, yet he felt it: There was nothing artificial about this playground mankind had been given long ago. Even the man-made structures on the shores fit in. He could barely see the little cottages when turned his head to breathe, but the people inside them saw him. He couldn't hear the families laughing and grilling pork on the porches of their summer houses, but he knew they were there. They were part of this world, just like Lake Balaton. The pool never was part of anything. Attila's world used to be 25 meters long, but now it felt infinite.

"It's like a light has switched on in my head," he'd tell his mom in the evening.

All the euphoria made Attila go too fast, so he ran out of energy and lost a lot of time on the last few kilometers, but he still finished as the fastest of the young swimmers. And for once, he didn't care too much about the result. He just wanted to go back and swim more races in the real water. This is where he belonged.

BACK TO BALATON

2007-2008, Hungary

After a week of "regeneration" – in other words: letting my body rest, laying on the couch, and pitying myself – I start looking for a boat for next year. I have one requirement: It needs to be able to stay out ·on the open water during a category-two storm warning. András Hosszu, a friend of my good friend who is also called András, connects me with Istvan Bodis, a local lawyer who has a few boats and rents them out sometimes. After explaining my plans to Istvan, he invites me to the harbor in Gyenesdiás.

On a late-summer day, I visit Istvan. I meet a generous man, a man that loves sports. A man that is on board with my challenge. "Don't worry about the money," he says when I ask him about the costs. Istvan tells me that he will provide two boats for me: A big one for the whole crew to stay on and a smaller one from which I'll get my feedings.

I surprise myself by how quickly I get back into training mode. Sometimes, my mind wanders back to the moment they told me I'd have to stop my swim. But it doesn't stop me from going through my training schedule. Again, life cycles through the seasons while I do laps in the pool. Most of my sponsors have stuck with me. They understand that last year was not my fault.

The winter and spring of 2008 are just like the ones in 2007, only with a few more mental battles.

I remember Nikos' words. "This will teach you to be much stronger."

I thought he was kidding. I had no idea.

Maybe I'm telling myself that he was right, only to make sense of last year. But it's more likely that…Nikos was just right.

He always is.

Fate played a cruel game with me, yet here I am again, waiting to start. I persevered. I'm about to prove that my actions transcend whatever life throws at me.

July 5, 2008.

I jump.

For lake standards, the water is rough. But then again, lake is not quite the right word for Balaton and its massive expanse. There's a reason we call it *Magyar Tenger*, Hungarian Sea. From the eastern shore, you couldn't even see the western end if there were no hills blocking the sight. The sun is shining, but 80 kilometers is too much for the dusty Hungarian summer.

I don't care. I've checked the weather projections. It won't get any worse than this. I'll be fine.

I go fast, probably as fast as last year, even if it doesn't feel quite as easy. But I won't let the conditions slow me down.

Only swimming. Here, I fell in love with open water. Here, I will triumph.

I fight.

For an hour.

For two hours.

For three hours.

For four hours.

For five hours.

For six hours.

My arms are aching like they usually do past the halfway mark of a competition. My lungs labor for every breath, sucking in the air as if I was doing four-lap sets in the pool.

So be it then. I am not quitting.

I pass Tihany.

Just after I leave the peninsula behind me, the water starts to calm down. Instead of a bumpy road of choppy waves, I now get to cruise along a silky carpet.

My shoulders hurt.

Who cares.

I swim on towards the sunset, Istvan's smaller boat right next to me. If anything were to happen, it would take me to the big boat.

I don't plan on needing either of them.

Night falls.

The lights coming from the boat bother me, so we try to

find a lighting setting that illuminates the water around us well enough for them without being a problem for me. It's the first time for all of us: Istvan; Attila, who will hand me my food; Zsolt, my doctor on the boat.

I've never swum in the dark in open water.

I don't speed up when scary thoughts creep into my mind. I must keep a steady pace; by now I'm pretty sure that I went too fast in the beginning.

The night is long. Plenty of time for plenty of thoughts. Except for last year's try, it's the first time I'm swimming a big event in Hungary. My friends and family have never seen me swim. Now, they do. And when the sun rises, they will wait for me on the other side.

So many of my friends are here.

As usual, my mom is not.

Dad could've just taken her on the 35-kilometers drive to see me race. "He will swim and come home," he told her instead. As if I was swimming at some random pool competition in a backwater village where only those who haven't made it into the bigger races compete, where neither time nor placement matters, where only the families of the competitors show up. Or rather, most of the families.

I hope she's asleep now.

If there was daylight, the conditions would be perfect. No wind, no waves. Not even the faintest sound from the shore. All the bars have closed by now. Only the boat's engines, my arms piercing the water, my legs kicking up foam.

Bliss can be found in weird places.

The sun is rising.

Surely, I've passed the halfway mark.

My body feels as if there was a thin coat of lead spread all over it, making every move just a little bit harder. On the bright side: That coat hasn't gotten much heavier throughout the night. On the slightly terrifying side: I've been swimming with it for 15 hours now.

Attila hands me my bottle with the help of a stick, I go get it and drink. Or rather: try to.

"It's empty!" I shout.

Attila looks confused. "Sorry! It's not feeding time yet!" After some more confusion, he tells me that he had fallen asleep and as he woke up, he thought he had missed snack time.

I shake my head and swim on. I wouldn't mind a nap myself, but those are thoughts I can't afford to have.

Just swim. I can only do one stroke at a time, so this is what I must do.

Feeding time. My friends encourage me to keep going, but I don't hear them.

The sun is shining, but I don't see it.

My triceps burn, but I don't care.

It's only the water and me.

I've reached my limits and I can feel it.

After 24 of the longest and somehow also shortest hours of my life, I know that I will make it.

I also know that the last four kilometers will be the worst of my life.

My exhaustion is reaching a level I have never experienced before. I probably could've saved myself a lot of pain with a slower start, but what's done is done. It's rare to say this in swimming, but today's Attila must pay for yesterday's Attila's actions. Every stroke feels like it's going to be the last, yet there's always one more.

And one more.

One more.

My body screams that it can't take it, no, it doesn't scream anymore, it blabbers in agony: Stop, stop, let it be over. It begs for rest. It feels deformed beyond recognition, like a towel that's been wrung out a thousand times too often.

My arm launches forward one more time. I can't stop after putting everything I have into this. After struggling for a full day.

After struggling for four years.

One more.

I know that I will make it. Once the body has accepted that it will have to carry me to the shore, all that remains is pain and time.

The closer I get, the more often I look out for the shore. So many people are waiting.

One more stroke, a little closer to them. In 15 minutes, I'll be there.

The pain stays, but it becomes more manageable. It's just a matter of time now. Ten minutes is nothing compared to 25 hours. And unless I made a mistake adding up the times I've been fed, that's how long it's been.

A hundred meters. This is where the joy starts to build.

For some reason, we are not headed towards the harbor where I was supposed to finish. As always, I stay next to my escort boat, and it leads me away from the crowd and all the cameras.

I'm sure there's a good reason. 50 meters. My body doesn't feel anything anymore. I do the last few strokes on autopilot.

I see people running over to where I'm about to arrive. I keep going. I put my feet on the steps leading out of the water and stand up. I have done it.

Now they know me.

Zsolt and Istvan jump into the water fully clothed. We hug.

For a little while, we're alone. Then people arrive. I recognize some of them. "Congratulations," they say. "Congratulations! Congratulations!"

"Can you go back and swim to where we were expecting you so we can film it?" somebody asks. "Bravo!" somebody else says. "Yes, can you go back and come ashore where we were waiting?" a cameraman asks.

All I can muster is a tired "no" and one of the slowest, most exhausted headshakes Hungary has ever seen.

Finally, it's over. Nothing else matters.

Nikos was right. It was possible. He knew how strong I was; I didn't. He trusted me; I didn't. He pushed me and made me push myself. Because he believed, I gave it a try.

The next few hours are a whirlwind.

There's a celebration. A press conference. Somebody wants to know if it was hard. It was. Zsolt and Andrea, a physiotherapist I'm friends with, check on me. Istvan tells me that he changed the finishing point because he didn't want people to see me coming out of the water like a zombie. Reporters from Hungary's largest radio station tell me that from sunrise on, they were broadcasting live updates every thirty minutes. Dozens of people tell me that I swam from 2.13 p.m. to 3.45 p.m., more than a full day.

At 8 p.m., I finally get to sleep.

At 3 a.m., I wake up. Wide awake, I watch TV until breakfast.

In the afternoon, I finally get to go home to mom.

THE WAITING ROOM

2007-2012

I thought all doors would open when I finished my swim across Lake Balaton.

Short version: They didn't.

Long version: I've lost some sponsors, but most came back after a year. I'm still struggling to get media attention for the sake of those sponsors, I still need to count every Forint I spend. But it's become much easier to believe in myself.

In 2009, I get an email from Steven Munatones, a true open water swimming pioneer. He heard about my Balaton swim from an American friend of mine and introduces me to a challenge – the "Oceans Seven". No, there is no apostrophe missing in "Oceans", that's just the name of the challenge. The Oceans Seven are some of the hardest swims in the world: Across the Molokai Channel in Hawaii, the Catalina Channel in California, the Strait of Gibraltar, the North Channel between Northern Ireland and Scotland, the English Channel, the Tsugaru Strait in Japan and Cook Strait in New Zealand. Last year, Steven combined those swims to create the pinnacle of marathon swimming. Nobody is even close to completing all of them, it will take years for the first swimmer to finish.

In 2010, I swim across the Baltic Sea. It's all just to warm me up, something to do on my road to getting stronger. I have decided that the Oceans Seven will be my destiny.

And a long time ago, fate decided whom I will start this

quest with. It came in the form of a paraplegic Australian whom I have never met and will probably never meet.

One lazy evening in 2000, I stumbled upon a documentary that captivated me like no other. The movie was about John Maclean, a former professional rugby player who was hit by a truck while riding his bicycle. The accident put him in a wheelchair. He was paralyzed from the waist down, but his arms still functioned. Maclean became the first athlete in a wheelchair to finish the Hawaii Ironman and then set his sights on swimming across the English Channel.

The movie was a showpiece of perseverance, grit, dedication, and hope. I was glued to the TV, cheering him on as he crossed the Channel. To this day, I remember what I felt like to watch his remarkable strength, to admire how comfortable he looked in the water. As he crawled out onto the beach, his physical limitations became more of an issue. He came to a sit on the wet sand, but that was not enough. Not for John Maclean. He pulled himself all the way up to the section of the beach where the sand was bone-dry, dragging his legs behind him. It was the most heroic thing I had ever seen. "This is it," I thought.

In a way, seeing Maclean drag himself out onto the dry sand was like swimming my first competition in open water. Back then, I discovered open water to be my future. This time, the documentary showed me how fulfilling solo swims could be. No races, no competitions – just me and a very long stretch of water.

Out of respect for Maclean's feat, I wanted to swim with the same organizers, the same boat. I could have gotten a window earlier in the season with other teams, but I didn't care about that.

In 2011, I get to do a very special swim. Lake Balaton is so big that it lies across three different municipal districts. The borders go across the lake in straight lines, so I swim along the northern shore and then along the border of my home district Zala. It's around 35 kilometers in flat water. Since it's one of the hottest days of the year, the water is 29 degrees. The swim is terrible. Whenever possible, my friends on the boat throw ice cubes on top of me. Badly overheated, I barely finish.

Not a single part of this swim is a good experience. Except one thing: For the first time, my mom gets to see me swim. My brother Istvan drives her to Balaton and she waits for me at the finish. I don't know if I've ever been more thankful for something.

In 2012, Mom dies.

She has been sick. We knew it was going to happen, so we all had time to say goodbye. During the last months of her life, I learned a lesson: I should have visited her more often. I never wanted to go because of my father, but I should have.

CHILDHOOD MEMORIES:
THE BEGINNING

September 1979, Zalaegerszeg

Attila's mom hung the key around his neck and told him to be home in time for lunch. Before she could say goodbye, he was already running out the door with a big smile on his face: Time to play!

He didn't even make it all the way down the stairs before running into some of his friends, Ferenc and Lajos. Their street was lined with towering apartment buildings and it seemed like every family living there had children that were around his age. Even if some kids were not allowed to come outside one afternoon, there was always someone to play with. Usually, they headed to the park with a football: They put pieces of clothing down to mark the goalposts and the whole park was their playing field. Attila loved it.

Of course, he had worries, too. The vegetables he didn't like; Zsolt, the kid who took the ball from him when he was about to score a goal during their last game, Szilárd, who threatened him after Attila had pushed his little brother Krisztián, and Eszter, who had asked Attila if he wanted some of her ice cream last Friday.

And his father.

THE ENGLISH CHANNEL

August 2013, Folkestone, United Kingdom

Apparently, the road to glory is a very long chain of highways that ends at a crappy hotel. It's cheaper for the three of us – my friends Andras and Viki are joining me – to drive up to Folkestone from Hungary than it would be to fly to London and rent a car, so here we go.

It has a strange metaphorical sweetness to it. This trip is just like my life: a long road leading towards this fresh start.

We arrive at Folkestone, check into our hotel – you get what you pay for, not very much in this case – and I get on with my training. Michael, the head organizer, spends a day with me and gives me lots of useful advice. Otherwise, we spend a few uneventful days, which is exactly what I want before a swim.

At some point, it becomes too uneventful. I agreed with the pilot, Reg, that he would call me 24 hours before the start. All day, my phone is painfully silent. It's not only not making noise, it has created a soundless vacuum around itself.

I must have checked seven or eight times if the thing really is set to ring loudly, even though I knew damn well that it was. Four times, I thought the light on my phone was flashing. I reached over, grabbed it, unlocked it. Nothing.

My morning swim calms my restlessness for a few minutes, but after the shower I'm back to counting the minutes and staring at my phone like a dog trying to steal somebody's lunch. I walk up to the local castle to keep myself busy, but all I can do is stare at the sea and ask myself: When?

I don't know how often I pull out my phone on the way down. I don't want to know.

Even if I can't swim tomorrow, Reg should have called already.

In the evening, he shows up. "Weather looks good, buddy. You're lucky. Get some sleep, we'll meet at the harbor tomorrow at ten."

So much for the 24-hour advance.

I call Zsuzsanna and Robert, my friends from London. They're going to take a day off to join me on the boat. If the pilot can't be trusted, I like having swimmer friends with me. They know what it's like in the open water, they know me and they know what I need. And usually, they're having a blast watching me swim, too.

I'm told they will arrive around 8 a.m., so I try to get some sleep. I've gotten used to the rock this hotel sells as a mattress; a t-shirt wrapped around my pillow keeps the sour stench of the pillowcase under control. It could be worse. Only my brain doesn't want me to fall asleep. 15 years ago, I heard of the English Channel for the first time. For three years, I've been training for this. Right now, I feel like I've been working towards this upcoming morning for all my life.

I don't remember falling asleep, but the next morning, I feel okay. Finally, the day has come. So long have I been waiting for it. As I am eating jam on toast for breakfast, Zsuzsanna and Robert enter the hotel's dining room. They left early in case of traffic, but their drive was all smooth sailing, so now they're here three hours before I'm supposed to swim. It's a joy to have them around, to talk about the old stories. I don't hear any doubt about my swim in their voices. That really helps. Keeps my own thoughts quiet.

I prepared everything before breakfast, so we arrive at the harbor just after 10 a.m. The boat is there. Reg is not.

Well, we had agreed to leave at 11.30 a.m., so we wait.

And wait.

And wait. I try to call Reg, but he doesn't pick up.

Am I having a bad dream?

I think of the movie Inception. "You never really remember the beginning of the dream, do you? You always wind up right in the middle of what's going on", Leonardo DiCaprio says in one of my favorite scenes.

Well, I know how today began and how I got here. Preparation, breakfast, car to the harbor. Not a dream.

So, where the hell is Reg?

At some point, I see him close to the harbor. I'm so insecure about my English that I have Zsuzsanna talk to him, but I understand the answer. "Yeah, sorry, I had to cancel today. We'll see how it goes tomorrow."

"What? You couldn't tell me this in the morning?"

"Sorry, I just saw that the weather wouldn't be good in the morning."

I prepared my food, my friends came here – all in vain.

This must be what swimming is like on the world stage. I'm paying a pilot to get me from A to B, like a taxi driver.

I've paid him close to 3,000 British pounds, yet proper communication was apparently not part of the package. Tough luck. Zsuzsanna and Robert stay for a few more hours, then they leave. They only had this one day off. I go to London with András and Viki for a few hours, just to take my mind off things.

After a dreamless sleep, I repeat my procedure the next morning: Prepare my food, have jam on toast for breakfast and go to the harbor.

Reg is waiting there. I don't even bother telling him how I feel about yesterday. My anger is mostly gone anyways, I understand that he is on my side and only wants to help me.

We go through the plan once more, but my mind is busy reliving the last 15 years. It has been a damn long road to this British beach. This place has seen so much: It was the home port for the Roman fleet in Britannia, it faced William the Conqueror, it was shelled by Nazi artillery from across the channel – and now it gifts me this peaceful, almost cloudless August sky, just for me, giving me a day in its grand history. At the end of this exhausting odyssey, I deserve it. All the years I spent preparing, pushing when I didn't want to, squeezing every ounce of strength out of my beaten body when I thought I couldn't handle another stroke, another kick: Now, they are paying off.

Now, I'm here and I'm ready. As I enter the water, I leave everything behind. Every drop of sweat, all the successes I've celebrated, all the hours I spent training – they don't matter now.

Now it is time to do my job.

In theory, the distance between Dover and Calais – or more precisely, Dover and Cap Gris-Nez, is less than 33 kilometers. But theory is theory, practice is…more.

The current will decide how far it will really be, but every swim starts with the first stroke. Then the second. And so, I swim, my mind clear of distracting thoughts.

The water is cold, but not too cold. The first few hundred meters feel good. I slowly edge to the left in order to get out of the way of the ferry routes. The ferries are to the English Channel what sharks, jellyfish or the cold are to other crossings. The Strait of Dover is the "busiest international seaway in the world", Wikipedia has taught me.

And that makes things very complicated.

Because of the strong current at the center of the strait, I need to swim a route in the shape of a flipped S or a question mark without the dot. Starting in Dover, I swim eastwards. Later, the current will carry me far south as I try to swim to the south-east. If I can do that for long enough, I hopefully manage to escape the stronger current and finish the question mark, followed by a turn to the left towards Cap Gris-Nez. To get far enough east in the first step, I must cross the ferry lane, once right after the start while swimming eastwards and then once more going south.

The safety corridor around the ferries is 400 meters. As

they are going back and forth constantly, there is not much time to cross their paths. My team needs to calculate the window precisely and I need to be fast. Passing a ship of this size too closely would force the crew to call off the swim, as they are required by law.

Yesterday, I wondered how I could trust Reg ever again. Now, I need to. And I do without hesitation, having left my anger and distrust on the beach in Dover. When Reg leads me across the ferry lane and tells me to push it, I do as he says, and when he tells me that we're through it, I relax. As much as you can relax in 15 degree water while trying to cross an Oceans Seven strait.

For a while, it is quite a pleasant swim, not much harder than the Baltic Sea. But after what must have been about 20 kilometers, a current brings even colder water, erasing any positive feeling left in my body. In the middle of the open sea, two degrees can be the difference between feeling a little uncomfortable and the cold ruling your every thought.

I am used to feeling pain when swimming. The human body is simply not made for what I do and my limbs are not shy to communicate that to me, but this has become such an everyday part of life that I usually don't even realize that something hurts until I've left the pool. The cold is different. It adds another distinct layer of pain, one that somehow finds a straight line to the brain. It is not more severe than what I'm used to, but it is more crushing in a psychological sense – maybe because it embodies a threat I fear more than pain itself: The draining of my energy until I freeze to my core, until my limbs refuse to follow my orders, until I sink like a rock.

When the cold comes, we choose: Will we persevere for glory, or will we be forgotten?

The Nobel Prize winner Imre Kertész, one of Hungary's greatest writers, had one of his protagonists, Gyuri Köves, express one of Kertész' core life beliefs: "If there is such a thing as fate, then freedom is not possible. And if there is such a thing as freedom, then there is no fate." Kertész took this insight from a suffering worse than any of us could imagine, his imprisonment in Auschwitz. Even in our incomparably easier times, it rings true forever.

In the water, I am free. Therefore, there is no fate, no inevitable success nor predetermined failure. So I choose, and I choose to swim on, and I repeat this choice with every stroke, sometimes more consciously, sometimes fully automatically.

The second jellyfish in less than an hour burns me.

Dusk is breaking. I have been able to see the shoreline for a while now. For us swimmers, it is common knowledge that you mustn't let your eyes trick you in the English Channel; even if you can see your goal, it very well may be hours until you arrive. Soon, this won't be an issue anymore. I will simply not see anything. I have never swum in the ocean at night. I loathe bodies of water in which I can't see what's coming – be it our trusty, muddy Lake Balaton on a June afternoon or the North Sea during a dark August night.

Having kissed two jellyfish already makes it even worse. While they haven't been all that bad, it makes me queasy thinking about what may come up. Hopefully no more of these transparent balls of pain, now completely unavoidable in the darkness.

But now is not the time to panic. I have to keep going, stroke by stroke by stroke. Every time I turn my head to the right to breathe, I see the sun slowly inching towards the horizon, slowing down for a final goodbye. She has done her job, shining all day, making her way across the sky like clockwork, the epitome of reliability. The sun would make a great swimmer.

As the sunlight fades, the lights of the periodically crossing ferries become the new beacons of the Strait of Dover. In the darkness, the behemoths of the water grow even more menacing with their piercing, bright eyes. For five calm seconds, I am glad that I won't need to cross their lane anymore; I completed the second, easier crossing hours ago. Going south, the current carried me. Besides the ferries and the faint light of the towns along the shore, a lighthouse periodically flashes its white-yellowish eye across the water. I know that it sits on the very tip of Cap Gris-Nez, not far north of where I am supposed to touch land. But now, it still is far to my right.

Trust the pilot. Trust the pilot.

Maybe I'm through the worst of the cold waters, maybe I have acclimatized: Either way, I am not struggling. Yes, it is cold, far from enjoyable, but I have no doubt that I will reach France.

I feel my arm touch something in the water.

Burn.

Jellyfish. It burns.

It is warm. Once the first shockwave of pain subsides, I joke to myself how lucky I am to have these convenient inconveniences offer their venom to warm me. I barely missed a beat, swimming as fast as before.

As I stop for my feeding, I see the lighthouse again. This time, it is to my left. I'm supposed to finish in half an hour. "Where is the beach?" I ask.

"We don't know," András says.

I keep swimming. What else can I do?

Just a few minutes later, a small boat detaches from the big one and approaches me. Reg's brother tells me that the shore is close. "Just go straight!" he shouts, lighting up the way ahead of me with a powerful searchlight.

The dark water is glistening where the light hits it, like someone wrapped the sea in tinfoil. Outside the light cone, the sea looks even darker to my eyes now, my pupils constricted by the brightness of the light. The white bright light that leads me makes me blind to everything else. A fitting allegory to my early years.

I do as I'm told: just go straight. Stroke by stroke.

As I can see the beach coming closer, feelings overwhelm me, satisfaction and pride permeating every cell of my body. A moment of pure fulfillment.

I have done it. Everything I left behind me when I jumped into the water in England comes back as a giant wave, and while some of the petty grudges lose all meaning, many other things burn themselves into my memories forever. The life-defining conversations with Nikos, the thousands of kilometers in the pool, dragging myself forward with aching shoulders and burning legs, the myriads of moments when I was on the edge of losing my patience: They all finally have their justification. I was right, I am right, I made it. This was worth all of it.

As I walk out on the beach after ten hours and 47 minutes of swimming, my elation fades.

I'm surrounded by darkness. No spectators, not even somebody sitting in a beach café, curiously watching. In my biggest moment, I am alone.

"It's okay, just swim back," I hear from the boat. Now there's someone that doesn't give the tiniest damn about what I just accomplished.

I feel empty. I know that I have friends on the main boat further back, but they didn't see anything. The most glorious moment means nothing if you can't share it with anybody.

I swim back, the amazing feeling from the last strokes having disappeared into a void inside my chest. But something remains. I have proven myself that I can do anything. I don't know it yet, but I have swum 47 kilometers. Eleven other swimmers have tried today with their own pilots, only two of us made it to the other side.

I can't put my finger on it, but something inside me has changed.

Joy arrives with a delay. It builds up like a wave as I am recapitulating the swim. When I travel back in time some 15 years, thinking back to the first time I read about the English Channel, that wave comes crashing down.

And just like that, it washes away the hollow feeling caused by the anticlimactic finish.

I completed the freaking English Channel! This is what it must be like to feel unstoppable.

Just a few days later, I'm even more thankful that my outlook on the swim changed for the better. My phone won't stop ringing: interviews, interviews, interviews. I am invited to more radio and TV channels than I knew existed. I'd rather tell their audiences an inspiring story than a tale of suffering and disillusion.

Everything will be easier now. I achieved something that is considered huge in the swimming community – and swimming is huge in Hungary.

In the English Channel with one of many ferries.

MEETING MÓNI

September 2013, Budapest

"Yes, it was tough, but that's what I prepare for," I say, probably for the 35th time.

"And so you did. Congratulations again, Attila, and thank you for coming," the reporter says.

And we're done. We chat for a little while, somebody from the backstage crew wants a photo and then I leave.

In a few hours, I'll do it all over again. Next TV channel, next interview, next "It was tough, but that's what I prepare for". Most interviewers ask the questions that are interesting to them. Naturally, those tend to be similar: how I prepare, why I do what I do, how my last swim was.

On the bright side, I don't need to prepare.

The break between the interviews is too short to go home, so I try to kill time at Mammut, one of the biggest malls in Budapest. I need a coffee, so I decide to finally give Starbucks a try.

Móni.

It must be her.

She is sitting at Starbucks. That face, that smile I fell in love with decades ago. I can see them.

More than twenty years ago, I didn't have the courage.

And now…I still don't.

What if it's not her after all?

I never forgot her. I tried finding her when the internet became a thing – nothing. When Facebook became a thing – nothing. All I could find was an address.

I thought about writing a letter. But what would I tell her?

"Hi Móni, sorry that I was stupid when we were young"?

"Hi Móni, we haven't seen each other in twenty years but you were the only true love I ever had"?

I couldn't do it. She was my biggest secret. Not even my closest friends knew I was still thinking of her. She was always with me, but invisible.

Now she is sitting right there. I walk a few big circles around the mall. I look at her from different floors.

It is her.

I act like I'm on the phone and walk into the H&M opposite the Starbucks where she is sitting. I feel stupid. No, worse: I feel like I'm 16 years again.

For so long, I have been hoping for this. Just a few steps now. "Hi, Móni. Remember me?"

I can't do it. I can push my body to cross an ocean, yet I can't get it to take a few steps towards this woman. The one that stands out from all the girls I've ever loved.

Fifteen or twenty minutes must have passed.

"Hi."

I don't know how I managed.

"Are you Mónika?"

"Yes."

She knows. "Do you remember me?"

"Yes, Attila."

Three hours later, we say goodbye.

Móni is a beautiful woman. She has twin girls. She is a fantastic mother. She has a good life.

She has a good life.

There's no room for me.

At least I get her number so we can stay in touch, the way old childhood friends do.

A HUNGARIAN REALITY

October 2013

How wrong I was. I thought that I'd be a star, but for the media and big parts of the swimming community, my success in the English Channel seems to have been a one-off thing. After the initial wave of interviews, the interest in me dies like a fish out of water.

For the sake of my hunt for sponsorships, I would have preferred a little more continued exposure, but I'll have to deal with this. My next success will mean another wave of interviews. And I'm already working on that – with more joy than ever. The biggest gift the English Channel has given me is the satisfaction I now get when I finish a training. It's one thing to imagine that everything will be worth the trouble; it's another to *know* that it will be.

After swimming across Lake Balaton, I knew I could trust Nikos. Now, I know I can trust myself.

LONG DRIVES

2014, Hungary

Tuesday evening, I text Móni. "I'll be in Budapest tomorrow for an interview. You want to grab coffee?"

There's no interview. But on Wednesday, we have coffee together.

Two and a half hours driving each way for a 30-minute conversation.

THE TSUGARU STRAIT

August 9, 2014, Honshu, Japan

The Tsugaru Strait is like a Great White Shark. Before seeing it yourself, all you hear are the horrible stories. Some are told by actual victims, but most of them are hearsay; stories whose details become more terrifying and exaggerated each time they are passed on. The ones who have faced the beast themselves tell the tale differently. They know there is no need to exaggerate.

The difference between the Tsugaru Strait and a Great White is that far less people have faced the Tsugaru and won that battle. David Yudovin first crossed the strait in 1990 and in the 24 years since, the number of finishers has risen to a grand total of…14.

I intend to be number 15.

And for that, I'm willing to suffer. I'm training harder than ever before: I swim 70 kilometers per week, and they feel even worse than they would do with a "normal" training program. I focus on my speed. That means swimming unholy amounts of 100-, 200- and 400-meter bursts to build up my base speed. And there are extra cycling and gym sessions. Fun, fun, fun.

To make it to the other side of the Tsugaru Strait, you must be fast. My friends have told me that if you can't reach the safe area close to the other coast fast enough, the current will drag you out to the open sea. Imagine what goes through an exhausted swimmer's mind: Eight hours of agony get you in sight of the coast and an hour later, you are an extra ten or 15 kilometers away. That would mean swimming ten extra hours. Try not giving up then.

The Japanese organizers told me that most of the swimmers try to save their energy and calculate for longer swims of about twelve hours. I may love the water, but I don't want to spend that much time in the sea, so I will take the fast lane. Full speed, no calculating.

Even getting there is hard. I have never been to Japan. There always were very few Asian swimmers at the World Cup races, so my only personal connection to Japan is my friend and fellow swimmer Yuko, who now lives in Florida. I had started looking for organizers a long time ago, even before I swam the English Channel. Few people over there speak English, so it took an eternity to get anything done. After countless wasted hours, I found a group that would organize my swim. I still have to book my trip and accommodation myself, but that will be a cakewalk. It's 2014, not 1994.

Hah. Booking a flight is easy, but trying to get the rest done from Hungary is a lesson in failure. In the end, I find a travel agency based in Vienna that specializes in Japan to take care of my train tickets and accommodation.

Getting on the plane makes me feel bad as always. The hatred of travelling that I nourished so well during my World Cup years has stayed with me and further grew as I got older. Packing my bags knowing that it will take me more than a day to arrive at my hotel is a grim prospect, but there's no way around it.

Japan.

The route goes from Honshu to Hokkaido, two of Japan's four major islands. Most swimmers stay on the Honshu side for practical reasons, but accommodation there is rare and insanely expensive. My financial situation is better than it was last year, but I choose to fly to Hokkaido and go to Hakodate, the biggest city on the coast of the Strait. More hotels, cheaper hotels. Staying in Hakodate gives me the additional benefit of being able to train on the colder side of the swim. You don't want your body to be surprised by how much colder the water can get when you've already been swimming for five hours.

In Hakodate, there is a long, beautiful beach facing the strait. Google it and you may end up at a CNN list of "Asia's 20 best beaches". The downside: It's forbidden to swim too far out. On a day with strong winds, the current's speed can be up to 15 kilometers per hour. A fast swimmer manages five kilometers per hour. And even on better days, it can grind experienced swimmers down. Once you stop moving forward, the current wins.

You get tired. The water doesn't.

Tough luck for me – I must swim. I must train, I must get to know the sea. Coming to a completely new place to swim is just like meeting a new person. Some bays you know inside out after half an hour, some are generally predictable but can still surprise you, and others remain an uncrackable enigma, even after spending weeks swimming in and analyzing them.

But every swim and every interaction with the water helps.

I swim twice a day: once in the morning and once in the afternoon. Different times of the day mean different tides, different tides mean different currents. Every swim is a piece of the puzzle and around the Tsugaru Strait, that puzzle is complicated, no, even impossible to solve in just five days. But at least my first trainings remind me of my top-notch physical form. All those 70-kilometers-a-week trainings have paid off.

After five days of training, my window opens – for just two days. Japanese marine and fishing laws are like rocket science and it was a challenge to find two days to swim. The organizers offered to extend the window to four days, but it would have been twice as expensive. I may be able to afford a mold-free room, but a four-day window? No way.

My friend Gábor, his son Mátyás and János have been with me for a few days already. They combine their vacation with helping me out during the swim, but for the training, I am on my own. The short window puts extra pressure on me. No training session must be wasted as I need to stay in shape. The weather is the same every day: Millions of raindrops flying in all directions, their feeble bodies thrown by gusts of icy wind. A rhythm, unpredictable yet steady. I don't feel comfortable walking into the water, yet I force myself to do it. No swim must be wasted.

I swim out.

At my usual turning point, I turn around and swim back.

Something jerks me away. A fierce current grabs me with an invisible hand and drags me down

I will die
Die
I will die   Swim
Swim
Die
Over
It's over

The whirlpool is a swimmer's most gruesome enemy and now this one has chosen me as its next victim. "You have no business swimming in these waters," it seems to hiss into my ears as I fight to stay above water.

I may never come back.

As this realization crystallizes in my mind, as it becomes real in the blink of an eye, I am swept away by fear. Two decades of swimming are worthless. I am helpless.

I throw all my energy into escaping the current. Waves crash into my face; I swallow gulps of salty sea water. I cough it out and inhale like it's my last breath. Another wave. Cough, spit, inhale, swim. Desperate rage is fueling me now. Moments of panic turn into seconds, seconds of panic turn into minutes. I don't know how much time I spend in that black fog, blinded by the helplessness.

But I stay above water.

And I come to my senses.

Keep pushing. It's just like always: If I am strong enough, I will make it. Stroke by stroke.

The helplessness is still there, I just pushed it out of sight. No matter how dark our surroundings may be – as long as you stare at that small spot of light, there is a way out. But even as I keep going, I feel fear watching me with an evil grin, waiting for a badly timed breath, a gulp of salty water that finds its way into my mouth, a wave crashing on top of me, pushing me under. If I give it even the tiniest of chances, it will pounce.

Stay cool.

I swim. With every stroke, the monster loses its grip. Confidence seeps in again, strength and trust replace despair. I don't know how, but it doesn't matter: I reach the beach.

This sea is rough.

I sit there and breathe deeply. The words "Stay calm!" have carved themselves into the core of my brain, the core wisdom of open water swimming now forever etched into my mind.

Back at the hotel, I check the data from my GPS watch. 400 meters in 30 minutes.

In the afternoon, I swim again. 400 meters in six minutes.

As if the chaotic sea was not enough, a new enemy taunts me all week. In Japan, he is known as "Halong", the "Descending Dragon". In the Philippines, they call him Jose.

Halong, Jose, whatever: a typhoon.

Even to us Europeans, the words "Category 5" ring alarm bells. Here in Japan, even more so. Halong has turned north after causing incredible damage while brushing past the Philippines. Now it is headed for Japan. And the Japanese meteorologists expect it to hit.

After my final training day, I have dinner. As always, it's pasta. I am eating with Gábor, Mátyás, János and two late arrivals: András, who will provide my food during the swim, and his girlfriend. "*Bazd meg*," Gábor and János say in unison as I eat my spaghetti. One of the nicer translations for that term would be "damn", the not so nice one starts with an f. My friends are staring at the TV screen on the wall behind Mátyás and me.

I turn around and all I see is a gigantic white vortex.

Halong is getting closer, and it doesn't seem to be diminishing. It's not even the only storm that threatens my swim, but it is the one grabbing all the Japanese headlines. Halong is projected to make landfall in the next few days, but that will happen in the South of Honshu, Japan's biggest island – and that should slow it down considerably. Still, a typhoon doesn't need to be that close to a place to make it utterly impossible to swim there. The winds can reach you even if you're hundreds of kilometers away.

A two-day window and now a typhoon. It is tough but knowing that it will be over in three days no matter what happens blesses me with a healthy portion of fatalism. It may sound crazy, but it is calming.

August 8: My window opens. I can't swim today. The organizers tell me in advance, but that doesn't make it much easier to digest. Half of my window is gone.

The Tsugaru Strait is the second-shortest swim of the Oceans Seven, but it's the one with the fewest people who have actually made it across. That tells you all you need to know about it.

Tsugaru doesn't do you any favors. There are no regular starting times, every day is different due to the ever-changing currents. "You can probably swim tomorrow," Masayuki tells me. He is one of the nicest organizers I've ever dealt with and what he just said echoes in my head like a beautiful song. "We have to start at four in the morning." Ouch. Not what I would have preferred, but knowing that a typhoon is coming, I don't mind the early start.

The timing is not the only bad news. The conditions make a start at Cape Tappi, the closest point to Hokkaido, impossible. We need to go down to Kodomari Cape – that's ten extra kilometers I need to swim. The pilot tells me that we have to take this route to be closer to the finish when the current hits me. As always: no second-guessing the pilot. Only trust.

Going to bed at 7 p.m. gives me a strange feeling. I sense the water reaching out to me, tentacle-like, whispering: Beware. This is different.

My mind refuses to rest, going over the strategy again and again, reliving the last months, swimming all those training miles in the pool.

Only 14 people have crossed the Tsugaru Strait.

The curtains are drawn, the room is dark, I fight to keep my eyes shut. But relaxation is out of reach, taunting me from afar. My senses are running on overdrive; every tiny sound is amplified by an orchestra.

Am I ready to be number 15?

At 11.29 p.m., a minute before my alarm rings, I wake up. It is a relief to stop having to try to sleep, but my whole body leaves the room wishing to go back to bed, not knowing how long it will be until I return. I have breakfast, get my bags, drive to the harbor: Some things are always the same, even at this unusual time. I barely talk. My insides are a mixture of tension, fatigue, and focus.

We meet one hour past midnight. It will be a long boat ride across the strait to the starting point.

Am I ready?

On the boat, my courage returns, pushing aside the tiredness. Yuko calls me. For a few minutes, she pulls my mind away from this cold Japanese night. "Remember: You're in very good hands. Don't worry, just jump in and push it," she says.

I am ready.

We are on the boat for hours, long enough for my mind to settle and refocus. Around four, it is time. I cover my body in a fatty cream to protect myself from jellyfish for a few hours, take a deep breath and jump. I touch the rocks at the starting point and start swimming.

No first strokes are ever the same. During the first few seconds of a big swim, you know if you have a good chance of succeeding or not.

Today, I do. My training has paid off.

My body feels like a bomb, just wanting to explode. I feel the power race through my veins. I swim fast – right on the edge of what I call my red zone. I could collapse if I stay in the zone for too long.

With each move, I feel how every meter I've swam in these past years has made me stronger. I'm unstoppable. Here in the water, I am the leader. I am the boss of my arms and legs.

As I plough through the water, the sun rises. This time, swimming at night hasn't bothered me. The memories from the English Channel are still very fresh, but knowing that the light comes in about half an hour helps. As the Land of the Rising Sun starts living up to its name, I get a better view of the boats accompanying me. I hear that they are happy with my performance so far: I am still going close to full speed, blazing along so that the jellyfish can't hurt me.

As I keep pushing my pace, I enter the rare state every endurance athlete dreams of. Some call it the "Runner's High", to me it just feels like a rush. Swim, SWIM, SWIM! Every fiber of my body is working to be faster than ever before. I feel one with myself.

Sadly, this cannot last for the whole swim. But even when the rush fades, I still feel great. Now, I finally see how good of a shape I'm really in. With every passing hour, what I believed to be my limits shift. Even when the wind picks up and the sea gets choppy, I'm surprised by how fast I can swim. For reference: A normal hobby swimmer manages a bit more than two kilometers per hour. When I check my sports watch, it reads 4.9 kilometers per hour. The Tsugaru record must be in reach.

CHILDHOOD MEMORIES:
HOME

August 1981, Zalaegerszeg

One of Attila's favorite walks was going down the street Mártírok útja. Just five minutes down the street and he ended up at the public pool: one indoor pool for the winter, one outdoor pool for the summer, the latter surrounded by a small park. In the summer, it seemed like every Hungarian came here. Sometimes, it was tough to find a place to sit down. Hungary has always been a nation of swimmers and there wasn't too much else to do.

In the summer, the swimming club held practice at the pool both in the morning and in the afternoon. When practice was over, the kids stayed in and around the pool to play until afternoon practice, and once that was over, they played some more. It was the same every day and it was a joy every day.

One Sunday had been especially great, the way only days in late August can be. It was one of the last summer days and the older people were getting sentimental, knowing that they needed to cherish the sun before it disappeared into the long, gray winter. Attila and his friends may not have been old yet, but they had their own version of late-summer anxiety: They got up even earlier and stayed out even longer, trying to squeeze out as many hours of swimming and playtime as possible.

But even those days had to end at some point. Attila made his way home together with Ferenc and Lajos, eager for dinner. Mom had promised him that she was going to cook his favorite meal: fried chicken drumsticks. She cooked a fresh meal every night, even though she worked all day. Attila's mom was a seamstress. She had been working in a factory for years, sewing together leather parts of furniture. After her second son Istvan was born, she became a home worker. The factory delivered a big machine to their home and from then on, somebody came with a small car every day to pick up her finished products.

For Attila, it was great. When he left to play or went to school, she started working and once he was back, she was usually finished. But the greatest part was in between: Whenever he needed something, he could run home, knock on the window, and ask Mom for it. Ice cream? Knock knock. Candy? Knock knock. Lángos? Knock knock.

She was always there.

His father wasn't, and he was glad for that. When he was around, he screamed a lot. Attila didn't like that.

THE TSUGARU STRAIT, PART TWO

August 9, 2014, Hokkaido, Japan

The boat is so big that it must be hard to navigate. Still, the pilot is doing everything exactly like I asked him to. Underwater, a pole sticks out to the side of the boat. There's a white band tied to its end and that band guides me at a perfect pace.

I've spent hours in the water, but inside me, it feels like the sun keeps rising. The water is cold, but this is where I've been training. No shock, just calmness.

Stroke by stroke, I can see the coast coming closer and unlike at the English Channel, here, it is no mirage, no evil trick the soulless rocks play on your exhausted mind. It must be two, maybe three kilometers away.

Something pushes me back. I fight, but it is stronger.

Another brutal current, storming out on the sea like a mad barbarian, swinging jellyfish-studded maces at everything in its path. Dozens of arms, a storm of power.

I knew this may happen; I have experienced it myself. For a second, the horror of my struggle during my training swim returns, but I quickly remind myself that the worst cannot happen here. I have company.

And that company tells me to swim to the side. A big half circle to escape the current and get to the shore safely.

That means lost time, but it's the only way.

As I keep swimming parallel to the shoreline, I feel the current carrying me away. It is obvious when it hits me, but much harder to tell when I slowly escape its grip.

Swim, swim, eat.

As always, András does a perfect job giving me my drinks.

I don't feel the minutes pass, but I feel the shore coming closer. I am about to complete my detour, the coast now only a few hundred meters away.

I feel safe.

I know I will make it.

Now is the time to fire the last bullets. Like a bull lowering his horns, I take aim at the shore and push myself. I know that the fastest time ever achieved on this swim is out of reach, but I can be second. Now, it is just like in the races when I was a kid in the pool. Only me, the water, and my competitors.

In spite of my exhaustion, a deep energy builds inside my chest. A gift from my body.

I blaze through the water. The coastline grows bigger, I can see a few meters of a rocky cliff going straight up, then a road running parallel to the sea. Behind it, a lush green hill.

On the last hundred meters, the boat stops, and I am on my own.

Once I see the rocks in the water under me, euphoria sets in.

The last meters. I have swum a perfect race, my body is completely drained, doing the last strokes only because there is no other way.

I touch the rocks.

For a second, the world stops.

I scream.

I hear the boat's horn.

My friends are with me. They have seen me.

I made it. I am number 15.

I check my watch.

7 hours, 29 minutes. The second-fastest time ever swum.

Thank you, Nikos.

I swim back to the boat and slowly climb on. Masayuki is filming, I give him the surfers' *shaka* sign: thumb and pinky pointed out. András hands me a towel. János sits next to me. They are exhausted too, but I can see the joy in their eyes. These are the moments I live for.

I am so tired.

As we go back to the harbor, I see everything that happens through a veil of exhaustion, but a feeling of fullness warms me. They tell me that I swam more than 37 kilometers.

To the harbor, to the hotel, to my room. Countless messages. All my friends followed my swim on Facebook thanks to Gábor's updates. I reply to some of them before a feeling of accomplishment carries me into a deep sleep.

The morning after, the wind is crazy. We go to Aomori and take the Shinkansen train to Tokyo. It takes four hours and between sleeping and talking to my friends, I have some time to let my mind get back in order. I know that I will not process everything until I am in Greece with Nikos, but I can start now.

We go straight to our hotel to drop off our stuff – and in my case, to sleep some more.

There was an earthquake in Aomori. We see the news after Gábor turns on the TV: Our Shinkansen was the last to leave the town. Afterwards, all public transport was cancelled because of the earthquake and the extreme winds.

Even though my mind is clouded by exhaustion, I can hardly stop thinking about how unbelievably lucky I was. Had all of this happened one day earlier, hundreds of thousands of Forints would have been wasted, my dream shattered, my sponsors disappointed, my future endangered. But Japan gave me one day and I took it.

We spend a short day in Tokyo and then it is finally time to fly home. At the airport, the crew of our flight to Paris comes out, congratulates me and gives me some gifts. We take some photos together just before getting on the plane: me in my plain t-shirt, swim trunks and sneakers next to the captain in full uniform. I even get to wear his hat for some of the photos.

There is no time for a breather. Once we touch down in Budapest, our journey continues to Zalaegerszeg, where the media and ceremony frenzy starts. But I'm in my hometown and I am enjoying it – I even had a Zalaegerszeg flag flying on the boat when I crossed Tsugaru. It's a beautiful August day, the kind that I surely would've spent at the pool 30 years ago. My friends greet me, I give a few interviews and the mayor personally congratulates me in front of the city hall.

My phone is constantly ringing, media requests flooding in every minute. I'm a one-man company, so I have to deal with all of this myself. I go back to Budapest for some TV and radio shows and enjoy lots of media exposure, exactly what my sponsors want. This is what will keep my dream alive.

After those few hectic days, I get to have some time for myself. Time to organize, sort receipts, think of new plans. My next two Oceans Seven swims are set, but I must plan ahead much further.

I spend less than two weeks at home before I leave for my other home: Greece. Kalamata to Koroni, 30 kilometers, the event I've swum at every year since 1991. But matters most to me: Nikos is there.

My coach is the one who helps me put everything into perspective. He helps me learn the right lessons from what I've experienced, he looks back with me, makes me close the last chapter and set my mind on the next one. When words like "You did great" or "I'm proud of how you have worked" leave his mouth, they go straight to my heart.

Next year will be the biggest challenge so far: two big swims without any time for regenerating in between. First, the Molokai Channel in Hawaii, then the Catalina Channel in California. That means a new training program and that's the most important thing I need to figure out with Nikos. But as much as we talk about swimming, he also gives me advice on other aspects of my life that are unrelated – or at least less related – to the water: relationships, friendships, family.

I don't yet know if my body will be able to handle two consecutive big swims, but I get a taste of what that's like in Greece. Less than three weeks after I did the Tsugaru Strait, I swim what feels like my home race.

Exhaustion and a supportive
János after my Tsugaru swim.

MY FIRST SECRET TO SUCCESS: PREPARATION

September 2014, Greece

I have won plenty of competitions only because I had better information than everyone else.

When I know how the weather will change, I can manage my energy better. From my research before the competition in Koroni, I know that the conditions will turn terrible after six hours. All the other swimmers start at a normal pace, I fall behind. "Be patient, be patient," I tell myself. "The weather will get worse. Later, you will need the energy to deal with it."

Almost exactly on time, the wind arrives. Waves crash into our faces; every meter becomes a struggle.

All the other swimmers run out of energy.

An easy win for me. As I am resting at the finishing point, I see the angry face of the Argentinian swimmer coming in second.

When I first started out in open water swimming, I never did this. Back then, everything came as a surprise – and surprises are the last thing you want in the water. They don't just mess up your race strategy, they also throw you off mentally. Now, I talk to the locals and check the data to prepare for a competition. Knowledge like this is a big part of why I believe that age gives you an advantage in endurance sports.

Weather predictions can only help me because I know myself well. I need to know my pulse at certain paces for certain durations so I can plan my swim. The more I train, the more data I get. Once I have enough of that data, it's easy to come to a good strategy.

But it's not just what the arms can do, it's also about what the mind can do. Sure, I suffer from agonizing pain during some swims. But I knew ahead of time that it would come. "It will not be fun. It will not be a party," I like to joke to my friends. What matters is that I have trained myself to give my muscles the directions to do what I need them to do, no matter what.

FINDING MY FOCUS

Spring and Summer 2015, Hungary

Japan has been a blessing to my career. All the media attention led to new sponsors, which means I can finally focus on my training and my training only. It's still Hungary, so money remains tight – but that's okay for me.

I stick to my plan of swimming two of the seven Oceans Seven races in the course of two weeks. It's probably not a good idea, but I can save a lot of money this way. First up will be the Molokai Channel swim in Hawaii, followed by the Catalina Strait near Los Angeles. Doing one right after the other will save me about 600 Euros in flight expenses compared to going to the US twice.

The Molokai Channel in Hawaii is my chance to break a world record. At 46 kilometers, it's a long and exhausting swim – perfect for me. I have told Nikos to extend my training plans. Suffering in the pool becomes easier when your goal is setting a world record.

I don't mind that my life turns into one continuous swimming training session. I can feel myself getting stronger and that's all I care about. It stings a little when summer arrives and all my friends go on holiday while I am doing laps in the pool, but I'll be happy about it by the time September comes around.

I'm not yet sure what my limits are and if a world record is really possible, so I don't talk about it too much. The only people I tell are my closest friends and the organizers of the swim.

With my coach Nikos.

MEETING THE GIRLS

Summer 2015, Hungary

Time to say goodbye.

I call Móni to meet up once more before I leave.

"I can't come to the city," she says. "The girls are with me."

"That's fine, then I'll come."

"Are you sure?"

"Yes."

I'm almost as shy as the twins when we meet, but everything goes well. A big step.

HAWAII

September 2015, Hawaii

On the plane again. Knowing I'll be gone for such a long time makes me feel like I'm leaving forever. I haven't been gone for four consecutive weeks since my days at the World Cup. For my third and fourth Oceans Seven swim, I even skip my sacred annual trip to Greece.

As always, getting through airport security with the feeding stick costs me minutes of my life that I will never get back. It's annoying to move around with it in general but having to explain why I'm bringing it gets especially tiring.

I fly together with György and his wife Melinda, but they stay in Los Angeles for a few days while I continue to Hawaii straight away. I don't mind flying the last leg alone. I'm just happy to get my feet off the plane, no matter how, where, and with whom. I arrive late at night, pick up the rental car and go straight to the hotel. It's a short drive, but I can feel my tiredness slowly crushing me with its irresistible force. As I pull into the hotel parking lot, I barely greet the security guard. I'm too tired to talk, all I can do is fantasize about falling into a soft bed.

If things only were so easy.

Tomorrow – or rather today, it is past 3 a.m. local time already – I will meet my friend Steven Minaglia for a swimming session. We've never met in person, but we've been in constant contact for a year now. He was supposed to swim the Tsugaru Strait a few weeks after me, but his swim got cancelled because of a typhoon. We agreed to meet in the afternoon, so I prepare my bags for tomorrow. As I finish packing, I decide to lie down.

.

.

.

Damn. It's late.

How late?

I check my phone. A message from Steven. Just one, that's a good sign. If he'd be waiting, it would be more. "Welcome to Hawaii! hope you had a good flight, we meet at Ala Moana for training. 2pm," his text says. He might as well name a random street in Beijing. "Hey Steven. I've never heard of Ala Moana," I text him. It's 1 p.m. in the afternoon.

My phone buzzes. "It's easy." That's all.

Welcome to Hawaii. Hang loose. No big deal.

Ala Moana turns out to be a massive shopping center, a city district and a beach. I'm still half asleep and get lost twice on my way there, but I make it.

At last, a beach. No matter how tired I am, seeing water makes me happy.

It's not a very Hawaiian day. Dark grey clouds are hanging in the sky like soaked cotton balls, I can see walls of rain falling not too far away. Behind the beach, huge skyscrapers rise. On a sunnier day, they would be sparkling in the sun, now they just look like two generations of a robot family next to each other: the ugly concrete high-rise next to the shiny modern skyscraper with the curved glass front.

A line of trees shields the beach from the robots, roads and nearby construction sites. I park my car and…and what am I supposed to do with the keys? I can't take them with me into the water.

I didn't want to leave my valuables in the hotel room, so I have around ten thousand dollars in cash – I still need to pay for the boat – and my passport with me. I lock all of it in the car and put my room and car keys into my backpack.

Steven told me he'd be swimming already, so I'll find him in the water.

I decide to just leave my backpack at the lifeguard building, one of those white huts on stilts that we all know from the TV show Baywatch.

The first dive into new waters is always a little special. We have ourselves a nice, refreshing swim and I get acquainted with the water.

Steven tells me that he is going back to the beach, but I feel like getting a few more strokes in. After all that time spent on the plane my body is happy to be worked out again. I decide to swim at a proper speed for a few more minutes and then take a quick video for my Facebook page.

As I leave the water, I see Steven changing next to his car. I head for the lifeguard building, but my backpack is not there anymore. I walk up to Steven.

"Did you take my backpack?" I ask.

"What are you talking about?"

"My backpack. The white one."

"Huh? No."

No.

Somebody stole my backpack.

Some godforsaken bastard stole my backpack straight from the lifeguard building at Ala Moana beach.

Some godforsaken bastard has stolen my backpack with my car keys, room keys and phone straight from the lifeguard building at Ala Moana beach right next to the world-famous Waikiki district of Honolulu. The only things he left are my flip-flops.

Damn.

At least my car is still here.

"You're not joking, are you?" I ask Steven.

He's starting to understand.

"That's so stupid. People steal everything here," he says.

But Steven wouldn't be a true Hawaiian if he knew the word "despair". "Don't worry, Attila, don't worry. Just sit in my car, we'll drive to the hotel, you can shower there and we'll come back to sort everything out."

"Steven, there are six cars here. The key had everything on it…the brand, the license plate…," I say. "How difficult will it be for the thief to find out which car the key belongs to?"

My most valuable stuff is still in the car – hopefully. I wouldn't want to be stuck on this island without my passport. And I don't even want to think about the cash.

I won't leave this car until I've taken my stuff out.

Steven helps me call the rental company, they tell us that somebody will come to open the car and take us back to the airport for a new car.

Steven offers me some of his clothes, but I don't take them. It's Hawaii. Even though it's getting dark and I'm wearing my speedos, I'm not too cold. Steven was supposed to pick his four kids up from school, but he stays with me. "I can't leave him here, all his stuff is gone," I hear him tell his wife on the phone.

We leave for the airport an hour before midnight. I walk up to the rental car office in my speedos like it's a perfectly normal thing. The workers laugh when they see me: "This is the guy that lost his key!"

"I didn't lose them. My backpack was stolen," I tell them. I pay a hundred dollars replacement fee for the lost key, but getting a new car is surprisingly easy. Hawaii is good. I go through the necessary paperwork on autopilot as jet lag is catching up to me. They could probably make me sign some stupid stuff if they wanted to. I get the same car again, but in white instead of silver.

As I pull into the hotel parking lot, the same big security guard from the night before lets me in. With a confused look on his faces, he recognizes me. Furrowed brows, head pulled back, eyes narrowed. He must remember my car being silver.

"I just didn't like the color," I laugh. He is still confused, but he waves me through. "Good night, my friend! Good night," I say. And I mean it.

This is not a vacation. It never is when I go somewhere for a swim. But being in Hawaii sure as hell is nicer than waiting for a not-so-totally-shitty day on the rainy coast of England. Here, I'm in paradise. Two weeks of ocean, waves and nature…I wouldn't mind if I had to stay for two months. My training schedule is down to two hours each morning, but I still spend most of my time on the beach. In the first week, Steven shows me three different areas of the coast. It's so valuable to have a local friend – not just for showing me the good swimming spots. I know I can rely on Steven in the water. Most of the areas are not safe to swim in alone, so when I'm on my own, I stick to Ala Moana.

When György and Melinda arrive three days later, my backpack still hasn't shown up. I don't care. I'm happy to have my buddies with me and I even received a replacement phone from a Hungarian friend who lives in the US. Once András joins us in three more days, we'll even go see the famous volcano crater Diamond Head. That's as much vacation as it gets for me.

The water around Hawaii is beautiful. And that water has sharks in it. They are the invisible danger, the one factor impossible to calculate. "Don't worry about it," Steven tells me, "I've swam here thousands of times and I've never seen one."

Sadly, that's not how fear of sharks works.

I know that there have been attacks around here. I've done my research. Yes, it's very unlikely statistically, but again, that's not how fear works.

As for the Channel, I still want that record. It stands at 12 hours and seven minutes. I know I can beat that. *World record holder Attila Mányoki* – how cool does that sound?

I remind the organizers that I'm aiming for the fastest time ever. They can tell that I'm serious. "That will be tough. If you want a chance, you'll have to swim during the night," they tell me. "It will be less windy then." Besides the sharks and jellyfish, the strong winds and huge swells are the biggest challenges of the Molokai Channel. It's never fun to be thrown around by waves, but you can't swim fast when they're three meters tall.

Most swimmers try to swim as far as possible during the day here because many shark species are nocturnal. During the day, people on the boat can spot the sharks, try to scare them off and get you out of the water if needed. During the night, I would be a snack.

But imagine: World record holder Attila Mányoki.

I talk about it with Steven during one of our training sessions. "Don't worry about it," he keeps saying. "Sharks! Sharp teeth! Worry about it!" my brain keeps replying. There have even been some recent attacks around the area where we swim, but Steven and I don't talk about them.

World record holder.

The organizers tell me that the weather will be good in three or four days, so I have to make my decision. I spend a lot of time discussing it with György.

A night swim it is.

The dark ocean remains a scary place, but I am slowly coming to accept that I will have to deal with it.

On the day of my swim, we take a plane to the starting point. We've been staying on the island Oahu, the swim will start on the western tip of Molokai Island and go back to Oahu. There are no ferries going between the islands as the waves would make it a rather unenjoyable ride. Melinda stays in Oahu because she is pregnant.

Hawaii is a slow place. We wait forever for our plane at the airport in Honolulu, we wait forever for the guy picking us up at the airport on Molokai and when we arrive at the starting point, there is no boat there. They're joking that the pilot, Mike, went fishing. He better be catching some breakfast for afterwards.

When Mike shows up, we realize that he has to stop the boat about a hundred meters from the beach because of the shallow water. Jeff, one of the organizers, comes in a kayak to get our stuff, but he's not taxiing us around. I can hear some *"bazd meg"* from György and András. Sounds like they were not planning on swimming today.

I get to stay on the beach for now. As my friends make their way to the boat in the late afternoon sun, I go through the swim in my mind. The Molokai or Kaiwi Channel is the longest of the Oceans Seven. The shortest possible distance is around 41 kilometers, but because of the currents, it will be more than 50.

I feel good, I am fit, I am ready. As Jeff starts paddling back towards me, I turn around and admire the tall palm trees painted golden by the late afternoon sun. There really are worse places to swim than here.

At 18.05 p.m., I jump in.

Throughout my swim, Jeff and Bill will take turns accompanying me in a kayak. It is compulsory here as the boat needs to stay quite far away due to the high waves.

I swim fast. The record is my fuel.

The waves get higher as I get out to the open ocean, but I manage to keep my rhythm. Feed. Swim, swim, swim, swim towards the sun. I want to catch it and keep it next to me, make it watch over me as I swim to Oahu.

The sun only turns red for a few minutes before disappearing. While the sky stays a purple hue for a while, the water turns dark instantly. My stomach twists into a big knot. I feel myself shrinking while the ocean expands into an endless pool of danger. There's a saying that the sharks will see you – the question is only if you will see the sharks.

But I don't slow down.

I can only see the boat every thirty minutes when they shine a light towards me to let me know it's time for my feeding. Bill and Jeff are my only connections to the rest of the world. Mike is in constant contact with my kayakers and tells them when to correct our course.

Being in a good rhythm is the most important thing when swimming. When I get into a rhythm, it's almost like the body does everything on its own. No effort, no thoughts, no worries.

Just swimming.

The sharks will see you.

I must believe in my shark deterrent.

My fear doesn't make it better.

Swim.

My pace is great. Jeff and Bill have rolled over a few times in their kayaks, but besides that everything is going to plan.

Around me, all I see is black. But I am flying.

Autopilot.

Minutes pass, hours pass, Bill rolls over, I swim, minutes pass, hours pass.

It's so easy.

CHILDHOOD MEMORIES:
THE EYE DOCTOR

1981, Zalaegerszeg

Attila's eyes did funny things sometimes. The other kids laughed at him when he told them what he saw, the adults looked at him like something bad had happened to him. Today, he went to see Alexandra's dad. She used to swim in the club with him, her dad was an eye doctor. They didn't have to go far; he lived in the same building. They just went to his apartment and Attila sat down on a chair between his parents.

The doctor opened a book and showed it to him. Attila had once done an eye exam for which he had to read letters from far away, but this was different. He only saw strange bubbles on this page. Maybe this wasn't part of the exam yet?

"What do you see?" the doctor asked.

"Bubbles."

"Can you read anything?"

How was he supposed to read anything? He could only see a bunch of bubbles, no letters.

"My teachers say that I can read well," Attila said, "but there is nothing here."

Alexandra's father started explaining something to Attila's parents. Attila's mom told him to try again, so he kept staring at the book, but there was just nothing there. "Trace it with your finger, it will be easier," his mom said just before the first punch landed on Attila's face.

And another one. And another one, and another one,

and another one.

"Stupid boy!" his father shouted.

Attila felt tears and sadness and pain. He wanted to hide somewhere and never come out.

"How can my son be so stupid?" he heard between the sharp cracks of a flat hand hitting his cheeks repeatedly.

The doctor and Attila's mom pulled his father away.

The boy didn't understand. He always knew why his dad was hitting him. But now, he didn't.

What had he done wrong?

OAHU

September 2015, Hawaii

I can see the lights on the coast. I don't know if Jeff and Bill thought I'd have a chance to beat the record, but now I'm definitely going to. I still have more than an hour to go.

I remember driving from Zalaegerszeg to Keszthely, the closest village on the shore of Lake Balaton, when I was younger. That was about the same distance as I'm swimming now. The drive always took around 45 minutes.

Swim.

The current often is an issue when you get close to the coastline. It seems to be the same here, as Jeff leads me in a line parallel to the coast.

I'm so close!

My lips explode. A wave of hell pours down my lower lip and sets me on fire. From one moment to the next, I'm engulfed in pain.

I want to scream, but there is no point in screaming. I check my lips. Jellyfish? I can't find any tentacles.

Time twists in moments like this. I don't know how long it takes me, but I manage to compose myself. The pain eventually subsides a little and I tell myself to keep swimming.

Swim.

My face

My tongue

Again

Time passes

Pain passes

Just keep going

The sun will rise soon. The sky is slowly starting to brighten up.

The next five minutes are hard, but I keep up my pace. Some damn jellyfish won't keep me from my record. It's time for my feeding – surely my last now. I swim towards the boat.

Fájdalomgyötrelemfájdalomfájpain

Pain

"AAAAAAAAAAAAAAAAAAAAAAAAAAAAAAAAA AAAAAaaaaaaaaaaaaah!"

I'm not swimming anymore. Only pain

"Uuuuuuaaaaaaah!"

All I can do is scream.

Words become useless. Nothing on earth can describe this. It's too much. The brain can't even begin to form a thought to grasp the intensity of this pain.

But it tries. I feel like a molten metal rope had slashed my body. Like a knife soaked in acid had cut me. I see a tentacle across my body and rip it off. It burns my fingers.

The pain is everywhere.

"Aaaaaaaaaaaaaaaaaaaaaaaaaaaaaaaaaaaaa aaaaaaaaaaaaaaaaaaaaaaaaaaaaaaaah!"

I've lost control of my arms.

All the air has been sucked out of my lungs. As much as I try to breathe between my screams, I feel like I'm suffocating.

I see lights pointing at me from the boat. They are searching for something on the water.

In between my screams, I hear them. "Attila! Shark? Shark?"

"AAAAaaaaaaaah jelly!" I scream.

It must have been a Portuguese man o' war.

The Portuguese man o' war technically is not even a jellyfish, but they do what jellyfish do: sting and hurt you. They are among the most venomous animals you could ever have the misfortune of meeting.

"Aaaaaaaaarrrrararrrgh!"

And their venom can be lethal.

I manage a few strokes towards the boat, I stop to scream, I manage some more strokes.

I didn't come here to die, I came here to set a record. I get my food and swim, stop, scream, swim.

The pain blurs everything, but I can tell that I'm still on a course parallel to the coast which is still about a hundred meters away. Why? Why am I even still in the water with how fast I've been swimming? Maybe they don't want me to break the record?

"You see, I could have done it!" I scream at Jeff. If they had only let me.

He looks at me calmly and keeps paddling. I can see him quite well by now, the sun is almost rising. I scream again, this time not at Jeff. I hate jellyfish.

Stop, scream, swim.

The boat comes close and Bill approaches us on his kayak. "You can turn soon," he shouts.

I. Can. Turn. Soon. The pain is still here, but it can't reach me now.

After a few more minutes, Jeff comes swimming towards us. "I'll guide you through the rocks," he says. Finally, I can turn towards the coast.

Oahu. It feels like I'm coming home.

The finishing point is supposed to be at a place called Sandy Beach. We are headed towards a rocky stretch of the coast, but there is a sandy beach right next to it. That has to be it, I guess.

Now that the shock of the pain is fading, my body remembers how exhausted it is. I feel like I'm falling forward in the water. Whenever I can save an ounce of energy, I do it.

The record. I can still make it.

I speed up. I don't know how, but I pull my strokes properly again. My arms feel like they weigh a hundred kilos each, but I throw them forward and drag them back as if my life depended on it.

The rocks are almost there. Jeff swims ahead and shows me the way through. I follow. I can't think much anymore. I'm like a car running on fumes and the warning light has been on for way too long now.

I can see Jeff climbing out onto the rocks.

Swim.

My arms weigh about a ton each. If I had to swim another kilometer, I would pass out.

I'm almost there.

Swim.

The rocks feel like gold.

I made it.

World record holder Attila Mányoki.

"Come on up!" I hear Jeff shout.

I want to sleep

I'll just stay here, floating in the water.

I stay here

From a universe far away, I hear Jeff laugh. "Come on up, we have to leave!"

It feels so good to float.

It would feel better to lie down. I'll swim to the beach. I'll stay there. It's not far.

"I'll swim out to Sandy Beach!" I yell.

So, I swim again.

Slowly.

I don't care.

Jeff is following me on land.

I walk out and lie down in the sand. I will stay here.

Time slows down. My body finally gets to rest. The gas tank is empty, but now the car is parked and safe.

"Okay, come on. To the boat," Jeff says. He is standing next to me.

I let out a tired, weak laugh.

The boat can't come to the beach, so I tell Jeff to call Melinda to come pick me up from the parking lot next to the beach. What a blessing her pregnancy is.

Jeff swims back to the boat. I have peace.

.

.

.

.

.

.

I have to go meet Melinda.

I get up and head to the parking lot. There's nobody around except three tall guys smoking weed. "Hey, they're looking for you!" one of them shouts as I slowly approach them.

"Who?"

"The police, the firemen!"

"What?"

"Where did you swim from?" one asks.

"I came from Molokai."

They stare at me like an alien.

My brain still runs in slow-motion, but while I'm explaining to them what I just did, I start to wonder why Melinda isn't here. I wouldn't be surprised if I ended up someplace entirely different, given how long I've been swimming alongside the coast. There must be more sandy beaches than the one called Sandy Beach around here.

"How far away is Sandy Beach?" I ask.

"Like four miles probably," the tallest one of them responds.

Damn. I have no money, no phone, nothing but my speedo, googles and swimming cap. How am I going to get there?

It's like they were reading my mind. "Come on, we'll get you there!"

They give me a bottle of water, put a towel on the backseat of their car and off we go. All three of them are high as kites, but I don't care. As we drive down the coastline, I see lots of police cars and even two ambulances.

"What is going on here?" I ask.

"Some poor guy went for a swim last night. Never came back. They've been looking for him all night, even had helicopters up in the morning," the driver says. "We thought you were that guy when we saw you."

After a few minutes, a car passes us in the other direction.

Melinda.

"That's her! She's picking me up!" I shout. The driver turns around surprisingly quickly, but at this pace, there's no way we'll catch up to her before she reaches the parking lot. Just before the spot we came from, there is a big hill. As we reach the top and start going downhill again, we see a police car parked at the entrance to the parking lot.

The driver slows down.

"Do you mind if we drop you off here?"

I laugh. "No worries. Thanks a lot, guys!"

As I walk down the hill, I see the policemen getting hectic. I'll have some explaining to do. Again.

Before Melinda and I start talking, we both let out a laugh. It's been such a rush for me and being with somebody I trust is a big relief.

She drops me off at the hotel and leaves again for the harbor to pick up the guys from the boat.

Oh, my sweet, sweet hotel room. How I've missed you.

I lie down on the bed, but just before I fall asleep, somebody knocks at the door. As I open, Steven stands in front of me, laughing and shaking his head. He has brought an IV and a selection of various creams and minerals as remedy against the jelly venom. I turn down the infusion but am happy about the rest.

"I was waiting for you!" Steven says. My tired face must be asking for an explanation, so he goes on. "I was gonna surprise you and join you for the finish of the swim. Waited at Sandy Beach, though."

Steven even dropped off his daughter at school a few hours early so he could be at the beach before 6 a.m. – but he never saw me. He tells me that Makapu'U, the place I arrived at, was the finishing point of the first ever credited Kaiwi Channel crossing.

"So, how was it?" he asks.

This is the first time I'm thinking about it.

"It was the hardest thing I've ever done," I say.

Later, I find out that I swam 54 kilometers in twelve hours and two minutes. Eleven of these hours were in darkness.

I broke the record by five minutes.

When I wake up the next morning, I feel how empty my body is. The pain from the moment the man o' war stung me is engraved into my brain. They say that if a herniated disc is a ten on the pain scale, a man o' war sting is a twelve. At least now, the pain is bearable. My lips are the only problem. Their skin has come off completely.

Something makes me take pride in having made it through four of these stings and not quitting the swim. The scars are like medals to me. Painful, ugly medals.

I spend my last three days in Hawaii resting, eating and drinking with Steven and András. Then, we leave for Los Angeles.

MY SECOND SECRET TO SUCCESS

"How do you not just give up?"

This is the one question I keep getting.

My answer is simple.

Quitting is just not an option.

I don't have a Plan B.

When my training plan for an afternoon session tells me to swim ten sets of 15x100 meters, this is exactly what I do. I don't give myself the option of maybe stopping a kilometer short. I have never done that since that one talk with Nikos that changed my life. The one way out I grant myself is an injury, but that has never happened.

If you get used to this in the pool, it is easier to stick with it during a competition. When jellyfish, high waves and sharks come together, your whole body instinctively wants to climb onto the boat. But mine knows that there's no point in even trying to make me give up.

It's easy to say, but it takes years and countless mental battles to get it into your system. But if you do it often enough, you can be certain of one thing:

You.

Will.

Finish. No matter what.

THE CATALINA CHANNEL

September/October 2015, California

There have been changes within the team: György and Melinda left, András is still with me and our friend Gábor has joined us. "How about we go up to San Francisco?" András asks on our first night in Los Angeles.

That's like asking a corpse if it would like to go see an opera.

"I don't care, it's up to you," I say. I know how much András loves wine. All I will do in the next few days is rest, no matter if it's here in L.A. or further up north.

He finds an affordable place in Napa, so we drive there all night. Or rather: He drives through the night, I'm sleeping.

Napa Valley. Sonoma Valley. Four days.

I'm sure I would appreciate these places a lot if the circumstances were different. Right now, all I can appreciate is a warm cozy bed – or something I can sleep on. András gets to try lots of different wines, I rest in lots of different vineyards. Once we get back to LA, I start swimming half an hour per day, purely for recovery.

I'm about to go for my fourth Oceans Seven stage. Never have I spent less time preparing my mind for a big swim than now. I don't need to remind myself of how hard I have trained for this; the trust in how much I've worked for it is wedged deep inside me. All these hours must be good for something after all.

The Catalina channel is one of the less complicated big

swims. Exactly 350 people have done it so far, with most of them finishing in around nine to 14 hours. It's about 32 kilometers, the ocean is around 18 degrees Celsius, cooling off slightly when you get close to the mainland. In short: This would be a piece of cake if I was fresh.

Swimming a distance like the one from Molokai to Oahu leaves its mark on the body for weeks. The next few days, I feel like I'm being tied down with rocks when I wake up. As I recuperate, those rocks turn to sand, sprinkled in every muscle and joint, still enough to make ordinary movements challenging.

It's October 5. Twelve days have passed since I stumbled out on what I thought was Sandy Beach. There's some sand left in my arms, but when I wake up in the morning, I feel that familiar rush that I wouldn't want to live without. Something big is there for the taking and I get to fight for it.

As I only start my swim at around 9 p.m., that rush won't carry me through the entire day. Time moves like thick syrup, one oozing slow-motion drip after the other.

I eat, I nap, I eat.

Drip.

I check my phone for the time. 6 p.m.

Drip.

I check the stuff I've packed again.

Drip.

I talk to Gábor and András again. I tell them that I think I can complete the swim across the channel in eight, maybe nine hours.

Drip.

We have no other topics to talk about.

Drip.

Somehow, we make it to the evening.

We meet the team at the harbor in pouring rain. From there, it's a two- to three-hour boat ride to Catalina Island. I've heard that for some swimmers, that boat ride already is the end – they get too seasick to even start their swim.

Maybe it is because the sea is rather calm today, but I don't mind the boat ride. I just want to dive into the water. As we arrive at the starting point, I attach the small flashing light to my swim cap. Thirty minutes past midnight, I finally jump off the boat and head back to the official starting point. Dan is with me on a kayak.

Go out, wave from the beach, go back in, swim.

After an hour, I am certain: I'm not rusty at all. I move like I normally do and things go smoothly, even with the currents not being ideal. After two hours, I still feel the same. After three hours, Dan is relieved by a different kayaker and everything goes to hell.

The relationship between the swimmer and the kayaker is very simple: The kayaker is responsible for the direction; the swimmer makes sure to stay next to the kayak.

It must be his first time doing this. Fifteen minutes after the change, I realize that I'm leading him while it should be the other way. No swimmer can swim a straight line in open water. It's perfectly normal to veer off course – that's why during nighttime or in choppy waters, when the companion boat is not reliably visible, there must always be an accompanying kayaker.

"We need to stay closer to the boat," the guy tells me. I agree and change course. We swim for a few minutes. He's next to me, so in theory, I should still be headed in the right direction. But I know better than to trust him. I break my rhythm and stop to check. I look to my right – nothing. I look to my left and see the boat.

It's at least a hundred meters away.

As I am forced to play the stupid game of swim-check-for-the-direction-swim, I start to feel the toll this last month has taken on my mind. My focus is weaker than it usually is. I can barely concentrate on my strokes with how angry I am. Normally, I would just push my frustrations aside.

"You keep swimming to the right, that's why we keep drifting away from the boat," he shouts.

No shit, Sherlock.

"If you kept the direction, I wouldn't have to worry about it," I shout back.

I start to get nervous. I don't know how long my stamina will last so I don't know if I can afford to lose precious minutes here. The night is surprisingly dark, the city lights of Los Angeles don't really help yet. There is nothing to orientate myself after but the kayak.

At least I'm still swimming fast. After hours of zigzagging, the kayakers finally switch and Dan comes back. The actual difference in my pace surely isn't that big, but in my mind it's a different world entirely. I'm finally making progress.

I still hate it.

I can feel my energy draining by the minute. Swimming to the boat for a feeding is a painful reminder of how little I've accomplished since my last drink. Swim, drink, swim, drink. The coast is still far away. The sun has risen. The swell is getting stronger.

At least I don't have to be on the boat now. I prefer being down here with the sea moving the way it does now.

Drink, swim, drink, swim.

Finishing within nine hours was a pipe dream. I know this because it is time for my nine-hour-feeding and from what I can tell, it must still be more than an hour to the coast.

I feel like I am swimming through a tar field. Every stroke is so hard to complete.

I move so slowly towards the boat that I arrive at the back of it, barely catching up. My friends with the drink are waiting for me in the front.

My brain short-circuits.

"Look how bad everything is for me! Maybe it's easier for you to walk back ten meters!" I scream at them. They rush back and hold out the stick with my drink attached to it. I reach up, but the cup isn't where it was a split-second ago.

What the hell.

Again, I reach up. A big wave lifts up the boat and with it, the drink.

I lose my temper.

"Okay! Just go to the beach! I don't care!" I shout and turn away from the boat.

I don't want to talk to these people anymore. I'll be fine without any drinks and food.

Any other day, my rage would make me swim faster. I would fly across the ocean, indestructible, purely out of spite.

I barely speed up. The fury churns inside me, but it doesn't empower my arms. It eats up my mind, but not a single ounce of it makes it into my empty legs. I slowly swim on.

When it is time for the next feeding, I keep swimming. I'm not talking to them again. I get some water from Dan and keep going.

I have never felt this empty.

I switch to doing breaststrokes. It's not a conscious decision, my brain is not capable of those anymore. I just do it.

My mind is a leaking pool of rage, anxiety and confusion. My body is a shell drained of its lifeforce, as if a supervillain in a movie siphoned every ounce of life from my blood.

I don't know how I keep moving.

But I'm getting there.

Some more water from Dan.

The shell that I call my body becomes even weaker. Every wave is a bouncer trying to throw me out of the club. I keep myself above water, collect myself for a moment and keep pushing forward.

My movements are fast considering my energy levels, but the currents are working against me. Hopelessness adds to the rage.

Back to crawling. There is no stopping.

Breaststroke. The coast is so close.

Crawl.

Nope, no energy for that.

Breaststroke.

The boat stops. That means I have a hundred meters to go. The coast is a flat beach covered by big rocks. It's not pretty, but it doesn't need to be.

I swim and the tide drags me out. The closer I get to the coast, the stronger the pull. In the pool, a hundred meters take me a minute and twenty seconds. Here, I've been swimming those last hundred meters for at least six minutes.

It's as if Yakety Sax from the Benny Hill Show was playing. I swim, but I don't move.

The only reason my body keeps going is because it knows that it's too late to give up. I'd rather drown than stop.

With every stroke, I gain twenty centimeters. With every kick, I gain ten. With every second that passes, I lose some.

I can see the individual rocks by now.

I'm getting close.

A wave almost carries me all the way to the beach, but the current pulls me back out again.

My muscles are tired of being on fire. I just want to do anything but swim.

Another big wave carries me to the beach and I crawl out onto it. I try to sit on the rocks.

I can't. I lie down.

Everything is colorless. Not even black, there's just nothing. I fight for air and close my eyes.

.

"Attila! Hey!"

I stare up at a yellow raincoat. Dan.

"Hey! Can you hear me?" he asks.

I nod ever so slightly.

Dan keeps talking, but I'm not hearing most of what he says. "I didn't see you move for a few minutes, so I figured I should come out," is the one thing that will stick with me.

He helps me sit up. "Stand up, buddy! Speak! You did it!"

He's almost yelling at me, but his words are coming from a different dimension.

I sit up. No happiness, just emptiness. After a while, Dan tells me that I need to swim back to the boat. He might as well just waterboard me.

I don't want to do this, but I'm too tired to argue. I walk into the water, so weak that the first wave almost takes me off my feet. Dan jumps into the kayak.

I don't know how I get to the boat, but I do. As I climb up, I can hear my friends cheering.

I'm cold.

I feel them rub my chest, feel that tingling sensation of my frozen body warming up. The sun is shining, but it's very chilly on the ocean.

I barely noticed that because I was so exhausted.

Still: no happiness.

Just exhaustion. I close my eyes and rest.

RESTING

October 6, 2015, California

I am free.

Although every cell in my body aches the day after the swim, I feel happiness starting to mix with my exhaustion.

I don't have to swim anymore. I'm free for now.

I'll never do this to my body again. Two swims in two weeks are outside my limits.

As I'm talking to my friends, the details of the swim come back.

"Did you really think we were pulling the drink away from you?" András asks.

Sounds like I have some explaining to do.

I try to make them understand that when you're frustrated, everything looks much worse than it is. Of course, I should have known that András and Gábor would never intentionally mess with me when they're feeding me – but out there in the water, after nine hours of swimming, after nine hours of mental torture, the brain doesn't work like that anymore. Thankfully, my friends understand that and don't hold it against me.

Later, somebody sends me the link to a news story about my swim. "The rain led to winds and unusually lumpy conditions. Luck was not on Mányoki's side," it says.

My final time was 10 hours, 59 minutes and 40 seconds. I can live with that.

Despite my growing elation, the terrible feeling I had gotten during the last two hours of the swim is still lingering around. Those moments are fused into every thought I have about Catalina.

I train hard for months exactly to avoid this feeling.

Maybe it was so bad that not even nostalgia will be enough to erase it. I hope that I can come back here one day in better shape. But for now, having completed the swim will have to be enough.

Four of seven. Three to go.

A VISIT TO THE ZOO

Fall 2015, Budapest

"Attila is so strong, we should put him in the cage with the lions and the bears and the tigers!" the girls squeak in joy.

We meet for the second time and they're already trying to kill me.

Móni finds it funny, too. I just hope this doesn't mean they don't like me.

I'm glad I decided to join them for a day at the zoo. Lots of time to get to know them, no pressure. Except for the danger of having to fight large cats.

Around noon, we cross a bridge over a little lake inside the zoo.

One of the girls takes my hand.

Maybe they don't want me dead after all.

THE HALL CALL

March 2016, Hungary

I'm ready.

Another tough training day lies ahead of me. I'm sitting at the pool, chatting with Sándor, the lifeguard. I tell him how my relationship with Móni has developed. Slowly, but steadily we've officially become a couple. In January, we spent two days in London together before I left for a competition in Hong Kong. In February, she joined me for a long weekend in Greece and cheered me on during my swim.

We're thinking about moving together soon.

Sándor laughs. He's known me and watched over me for an eternity. I remember when he took me to my first open water competition. Sándor may be 55 years now, but his personality hasn't changed. Helpful and joking, just with a few more wrinkles in his face.

My phone rings. I jump out of the water and pick up. "Hello?"

"Hello, is this Attila Mányoki?"

I've never heard this voice before.

"Yes."

"My name is Ned Denison."

This guy is a legend in open water swimming.

"Yes, hello!"

"Attila, I have some good news for you. You have been selected for the International Marathon Swimming Hall of Fame."

"YAAAAAAAAAAAAAAAAAAAAAAAAAAAAAAA
AAAAAAAAAAAAAAA"

THIS IS FANTASTIC

"IGEEEEEEEEEEEEEEEEEEEEEEEEEEEEEE
EEEEEEEEEEEEEEEEEEEEEEEEEEEEEEEEEE
EEN," I scream while the phone is still on. Ned is getting a free lesson in some basic Hungarian.

I've never celebrated anything like this. Once I'm out of breath and end my victory roar, I finish my phone call with Ned. He tells me that there will be an induction ceremony in the US.

Sándor looks at me with a huge smile. "You screamed for three minutes," he laughs.

Chasing recognition at home is a fruitless venture because so few people here know the intricate ins and outs of my sport – the challenges, the hard times one faces, how few succeed. Being chosen for the Hall of Fame means that those who truly know what it takes deem you worthy to join their ranks. Only the results matter to the selection committee. Nobody gets in just because they are somebody's friend.

UP NORTH

Summer 2016, Northern Ireland

I acclimatize to the cold water by joining Ned Denison's Cork Distance Week, a nine-day boot camp for ultra-endurance swimmers. Finally, I'll meet the guy who gave me the Hall of Fame news in person. Ned is one of marathon swimming's biggest legends. His training camp puts participants through hell: waves, temperature changes, swimming down a rapid stream, boats spraying you with water, Ned screaming at you, fellow swimmers struggling to do one more stroke – Cork has everything.

As I board the plane back to Hungary, I wished I had more money so I could just stay here in the cold the entire month until my swim in Northern Ireland. But I've got to spend three weeks at home. And that's three too many. Hungary's summer can be very hot. With every day I spend at home, rushing from sponsor meetings to training sessions to family duties, I can feel my body's resistance to the cold crumbling. A cold shower is cold again. The pool feels frighteningly normal instead of oddly warm. Turns out getting sunburnt in 35-degrees weather can reverse back your body's acclimatization at lightning speed.

When I touch down in Belfast, I feel like I've been dropped straight into Siberia.

For the first time, Móni joins me for a swim. It's just for a few days during the preparation for my crossing of the North Channel, but it gives me an amazing feeling. As we climb up the stairs to board the plane, I feel like we're taking a big step in our relationship.

Also, I'm glad to have her with me for a very practical reason: Her English is much better than mine. I'm fine in the US or in London, but the Northern Irish accent is a different challenge. That much I've learned during the training camps.

We arrive at the Northern Irish coast and I take her to my first meeting with my pilot.

After thirty seconds, I know two things: One, I can understand him just fine. Two, I'd rather not.

"Whoever comes here to swim is stupid," he says. "I don't care who you are. You give me the money, I bring you to Scotland."

Móni and I rarely agree as much as we do now: We're uncomfortable. I didn't expect to meet a new best friend here, hell, I still remember how many emails I had to write just to get him to reply. But I had put that down to him being an old man. From the locals, I learn that he used to be a fisherman, then started providing fishing trips for tourists, and as demand for channel crossings rose, he moved to that. In short: He's following the money.

But I hired him and the sea is the same no matter who pilots the boat.

I don't have to wait long for the next shock. When I hit the ocean to train for the first time, it is much colder than I expected. As I get out of the water after an hour-long training session, Móni looks like she's seeing a ghost.

I guess I'd do the same if I saw myself shake this uncontrollably.

Over the next few days, I can sense that she is worried. As for myself…I remain more nervous than I usually am.

Most things are fine – the accommodation, the locals, even the food – but my pilot's casual taxi-driver-esque mentality and how cold I am in the water make me uneasy.

I don't know many swimmers here, so I train alone for the first few days.

After Móni leaves, András, his girlfriend Adrienne, and János join me.

My Greek friend Charis is scheduled to swim around the same time as I am. He'll swim with the Infinity crew. I train with him a few times and a few more times with two other swimmers who will attempt the crossing: Steve from the US and Shubham from India. We all agree on one thing: It is cold.

My window opens and I've regained confidence. I remember that I've swum the fastest time of the 2013 season at the English Channel, I hold the second-fastest time ever in Japan, I've set the record in Hawaii and I survived Catalina twelve days after that.

Here, I wouldn't care about the time all that much – if it wasn't for me trying to get out of the water as fast as possible. I haven't even been here for a week, so the sea still feels like a pool of ice to me.

On Friday, I get the call: "Come for the final meeting, you swim tomorrow."

When I talk to Charis, he says that he probably won't swim tomorrow. His organizer Padraig doesn't like the conditions.

That's a little worrying, but I must focus on myself. Four out of four Oceans Seven swims so far. Time to make it five out of five.

My mind is running in circles, but I manage to get some sleep.

CHILDHOOD MEMORIES:
SWIMMING

1983, Zalaegerszeg

It felt good to be fast in the pool. All Attila heard from his father was how stupid he was, how he would never be anybody, how he always messed things up. When he swam, he was doing something right.

At school, he struggled with some subjects. Whenever Attila had problems with a teacher, he stopped trying. Those teachers would tell his parents that their son was "minimalist". "They leave out that they treated me badly before I stopped working hard," Attila would complain to his parents. He was great at math. He loved his teacher, Ms. Ludanyi, she was like a grandmother to the kids.

But swimming was even better than math. It had been three years since Attila joined the club because the doctor had told his mom that it would be good for his asthma. He still struggled with the sickness, especially during training – but he was happy that it got him into swimming.

On some weekends, they had competitions. Attila hadn't won a medal yet, but he had come close a few times.

Sadly, Attila's mom usually couldn't come to his races because she was cooking and taking care of the house. That day, he was happy that at least his father and his older brother Istvan were there.

As always, his only race was the 50 meters freestyle.

Just two lengths of the pool. Short enough to go full speed without worrying about stamina.

As he jumped into the water, he knew that it was a great start. He sped to the other side and back as fast as he could.

He looked around. Nobody had finished before him.

"I won!" Attila thought.

He felt like a champion.

When he started jumping in circles, one of the coaches told him that there had been too many swimmers to all fit them in one heat, so his time only was the third-fastest.

"A medal! I won my first medal!" he celebrated, still feeling like a champion.

After Attila had received his medal, he ran to Istvan and his father. Istvan was happy too, but his dad gave him a surprised look. "Why are you so happy? You are just third," he said.

NORTH CHANNEL I

August 13, 2016, Northern Ireland

7 a.m., time to swim. From the harbor it's a short cruise to the starting point.

As we arrive, I see that Shubham will be starting right after me. I think he has a very real shot at finishing. Being just 20 – or even 19? – years old is a big challenge in tough swims like this one, but he is incredibly fit and well-prepared. I got to know him during the Cork Distance Week, he's been staying in Ireland ever since and won a Gold medal at the Irish Open Water National Championships.

None of that will get him to the other side though. Now, it's only us and the sea. And the wind. And those godforsaken waves.

The procedure is the same as always, no matter what the crew is like. Put on some protective grease, warm up the shoulders, jump in the water. And, as always: Trust the pilot.

Five out of five.

András, János and Adrienn send me off with a cheer. The water hits me like a wall of ice. I wasn't expecting to jump into a warm bowl of soup, but this is worse than I feared.

Another reason to hurry.

I try to get into a rhythm. Stroke by stroke, I get closer to Scotland. My first feedings go well, but what I see in the sky gives me little hope for better weather: I can neither see the sun nor any holes in the thick blanket of clouds.

There are dozens of smart quotes about how humans can get used to anything. That's because it's true.

After a few hours, I barely feel the cold. I swim, I drink, I navigate the chaotic waves, I swallow some sea water, I swim.

It's cold, but I'm not cold.

Or maybe I *am* cold, but I just don't notice it.

"It's not good today," the pilot says. "There's no chance anybody is going to finish today. Better to just give up."

I've been in this frozen puddle of hell for four and a half hours and now, my pilot tells me to quit. I take an extra second to finish my drink.

"It's okay. I'll try."

I can see he is about to say something.

"I'll try! I'll try!" I shout before swimming away.

Five out of five.

It's not like the pilot was lying when he said that the conditions weren't good. They're bad. There is no sun, the sea is choppy, but for some reason the jellyfish are still coming up to the surface. They're not supposed to do that with waves like that, but I've lost count of how many I've touched.

Every gust of wind cools down my back a little more, every wave is another small, but hard slap to my system.

During my next feeding, I don't bother getting into a conversation. I wolf down my energy drink and swim on.

I can see the coast getting closer.

The next feeding comes. Same procedure.

Swim, swim, swim.

I swallow cold, salty water when a wave hits me just as I turn my head to breathe. My own mind takes the opportunity to backstab me: "The pilot probably was right," it tells me for a second.

It's really cold.

Swim.

I can see Scotland.

WAKING UP

August 13, 2016, Scotland

"Attila?"

"Attila? Hey!"

It feels like this is not the first time this voice has said my name.

I open my eyes.

I'm in a hospital bed.

I feel like I just woke up from a nap that was a little too short. I'm still exhausted, but okay.

I don't remember making it to the other side.

I'm surprisingly okay with that. I feel so calm.

I must have swum until my body couldn't go on. It wasn't me giving up, it was my body shutting down.

I can truly say that I went to my limit.

After a few slow breaths, I ask the voices around me what happened.

"What do you remember?" somebody asks.

"Swimming…and then I guess I fell asleep because I was so tired?"

"You fell unconscious," the voice says. I know the voice, but my brain doesn't have the capacity to connect it to a face right now. "Your body was too cold."

The voice hesitates.

"Attila, you are very lucky to be alive."

Wow. I take a deep, heavy breath. And one more.

My soul is full of pride.

I didn't quit. I reached my limit.

After all that training, I never knew if I could really do it.

How many people can say this about themselves?

Poets used to write about how you can be willing to die for your love or your nation. In the past, many people lived this way. Today, those words are empty. It sounds good, but few people do it. In times long gone, they truly believed in it.

The voice – I now realize that it belongs to András – makes a weird sound, like it is trying to clear its throat.

"We called Móni," he says.

Móni.

Damn.

I feel like I'm in free fall. I haven't thought about her at all.

It must have been terrifying for Móni to get that call. All my life, I'm trying to make others happy. Now, I've done the exact opposite.

I didn't spend a single second thinking of my family the entire time I was swimming. It was only me, the water and the other side. I was ready to die.

Or I didn't consider it possible. I'll never know.

Over the next few minutes, I get the short version of my last few hours: After seven hours of swimming – I only remember six of them – I fell unconscious and was pulled out of the water. Severe hypothermia, they say. A doctor was flown to the boat by helicopter to stabilize me, an ambulance was waiting for me on the coast to bring me to the hospital. They warmed up my body and woke me up. Shubham was pulled out of the water unconscious as well. He's doing okay.

"When did you feel that it was cold?" the doctor asks me out of the blue.

I laugh.

"When I jumped into the water!"

After around four hours, they let me go. The boat ride back to Northern Ireland gives me a lot of time to think. I'll come back here.

The next day, Keith Garry from Ireland sets the men's record for a North Channel crossing in nine hours and 57 minutes. What a difference having the patience to wait one more day can make. Next year, I'll go with a different crew.

Another day later, I go for a swim with Shubham. The sun is shining, not a single cloud in sight. What a difference waiting two more days would have made. Next year, I'll most definitely go with a different crew.

HOME AGAIN

August 2016, Hungary

After two more days in Bangor, I board my scheduled flight back to Hungary.

Once I get home, the moment I've been dreading arrives. Móni tells me about the call she got from the hospital. She says it went like this: "Attila is in a coma. They're trying to revive him. Do you know his insurance information? Okay, bye."

I feel so guilty.

"I was stuck here. There was nothing I could do," Móni says in between cries.

She takes a second to wipe away the tears. I don't know what to say.

"You are gone and we are here waiting for you," she says with desperation in her eyes.

Part of me wants to tell her that this will never happen again. But I am an honest man. "Móni, my love. I don't want to make you feel this way ever again," I say, "but I can't know where this limit is."

It's always one more stroke, one more breath, one more kick, one more stroke, one more, one more, one more. In the water, I have to believe that I am unstoppable! If I quit as soon as things become hard, I have no chance at success. This is why I can't promise Móni anything.

SHARKS AND SNORKELS

Winter/Spring 2017, Hungary

"Of course, I will wear my shark protector," I tell Móni. I don't tell her that I'm only doing it for her and the girls' sake. For me, it's just extra weight. The protectors are supposed to keep sharks away by giving off an electrical current, but you can't test their effectiveness on every shark. There's a reason why none of the manufacturers give you a guarantee. But putting this small black box on my wrist is the least I can do for Móni and the girls. That and not telling them anything about my research.

That research is thorough as always. Of all the Oceans Seven crossings, the Cook Strait between New Zealand's North and South Island is where you are most likely to encounter a shark. I've spent dozens of hours looking at shark attack maps: Where there were provoked attacks, where there were unprovoked attacks, how badly the victims were injured. I don't do this to give myself an extra push or because I enjoy toying with my own fear – it's just another part of my preparation. Just as I need to know where the dangerous currents are, I need to know my odds of running into a wall of pointy teeth.

Out there in the water, I don't need any bad surprises. Knowing that there are unholy amounts of sharks roaming the sea prepares me for them. If I see one – which wouldn't necessarily amount to an attack, life is not a Hollywood movie – I will be able to stay calm.

Once I'm done with my shark research, I barely think

about it anymore – except for when I'm being interviewed. The shark questions come up every time. "Are you worried? What do you do to protect yourself? Is this your most dangerous swim?"

And while I would love to answer all these questions with a frank "I don't care", it wouldn't quite be the truth. I know the risks and I accept them: If a shark wants to kill you, it does. It is bigger, stronger and faster than you. Worrying about it doesn't give you a better chance at survival. Once I was in the water in Hawaii, I wasn't too worried about sharks. I don't plan to spend mental energy on thinking about them in New Zealand, either.

Sharks are not even the only danger in the waters of Cook Strait. The currents are treacherous and the jellyfish plentiful.

That's why I work so much harder and swim so much faster than others. I could easily swim this in nine hours with much less training. But I don't want to be in that shark- and jellyfish-infested water for nine hours if it's possible to be out in seven hours. "The faster you get up the mountain, the shorter it is painful," the cyclist Marco Pantani wrote in his biography. It is one of my favorite books.

For six months, I train with a special snorkel. It's modified to purposefully let in less air. It also lets in some water, so that I have to breathe out strongly. That works out the muscles around my ribs. When these muscles need to work overtime in New Zealand, they'll last longer. A bonus: About a month before the swim, I'll stop using the snorkel – and then, it'll be like swimming with a turbo on.

CHILDHOOD MEMORIES: LEAVING HOME

1989, Zalaegerszeg

The swimming pool closed. "It's too old," they said and announced that reconstruction would take three years. The lanes where Attila had swum so many kilometers in were emptied, his club would have to shut down. There was no reason to have a swimming club when there was no place to swim.

Everybody had known that the pool was in terrible condition. But it had been like this forever. Attila had thought that they would let them swim for a few more years and so did most of his peers. He was still far too short to be a national champion, but he knew that he could achieve *something* in this sport. Maybe he would be a late bloomer and grow tall, or maybe he'd find another way to be better than the others.

But not without a pool. He would have to look for a new dream.

"We want you to come to Budapest," the man who had introduced himself as Mr. Azanger said. "We will give you the chance to train there. You have potential for open water."

"What?" Attila thought.

He was just 16 years old; he'd only been to Budapest a few times for national championships, it was a big city far away from home, he didn't know if he'd be good enough to train there. All of this scared him.

But not as much as his father.

There wasn't much Attila was leaving behind in Zalaegerszeg. He'd lost touch with Móni two years before. "He's in love," his friends had kept saying…Attila had to tell them that he was not. They had never been together, so there was no official breakup. No "Attila, it's over" like in the movies. No tears. Attila didn't know if Móni understood his problem and he didn't realize how far ahead of him she was in her personal development. It was just the time where the difference between girls and boys is the largest. Either way, they were not talking to each other anymore.

So, Budapest?

"Try it, sweetheart," his mom said.

His dad? "Go ahead, you will fail and come back anyways."

"When can I move?" Attila asked. The following Monday, he could start training in Budapest, more than 200 kilometers away from home.

There was not much time for goodbyes. Mom helped him pack all his clothes and swimming stuff and he met up with his closest friends one last time.

Attila could barely sleep during his last night in Zalaegerszeg. Tossing and turning in his bed, he started to understand what this meant for his life. He'd get away from his father's abuse and from this small town where every big dream is considered a mistake, where the walls around people's imagination are made of stone instead of glass. He was so excited that he sat up on the edge of his bed, letting his legs dangle like a five-year-old about to go to Disneyland.

Attila saw how sad it made his mom to see him leave, even if she tried to hide it. But as much as it hurt her, her son knew that she supported him. His father didn't seem to care. When they said goodbye, he asked: "When will you come back?"

"Never, I hope," Attila replied.

He was about to conquer the world. And he had just beaten his first big opponent.

LEAVING FOR NEW ZEALAND

March 2017, Hungary

Almost dying hasn't made my discussions with Móni easier.

"To me, the guy that climbed four eight-thousanders and lives is the winner. Not the one that climbed eleven and dies at the twelfth," she says.

I understand her worries. But I can't stop.

"Look, twenty years later, when he retires, he will have less peaks than the other one. Because he has the mentality of turning back!" I retort.

"But he's alive!"

"He's dead or alive, nobody cares! The other achieved more," I plead with her. When people tell me that I'm a winner just for making it back…who cares? When I actually achieve something, that's when people will care. Even if I spend a few days in a hospital afterwards.

We will never see this the same way. What matters is that Móni accepts the way I see things and still loves me.

NEW ZEALAND

March to April 2017, New Zealand

"You can't swim", Philip says. "The conditions just aren't good enough."

Today is the last day of my window. Coming home empty-handed could end my dream. I have invested five million forint – more than 16.000 US dollars – in this trip, all received from my sponsors. They wouldn't want me to come home without something to show for their money…again. Last time, at least I brought home a good story. I'd rather try and fail than not try at all.

If my sponsors abandon me, coming back next year is not going to happen. "Can I get a new window now?" I ask.

Everything is negotiable. I get two more weeks in April, the last of the season. I change my flight tickets, find a new accommodation, move all my stuff there. I don't mind. I have my dream back.

Twenty-one training days, get into the water, cross the strait, get out of the water, go home, kiss Móni, play with her daughters, relax. That was a good plan. Yet, here I am three weeks later, knowing that I have to stay. "How nice, you had a long vacation in New Zealand!" some people will tell me. They always do.

I hope none of them spend their vacations like this.

To me, New Zealand is a stretch of road about 1,500 meters long. It's the one going from the hotel to the bay, from the bay to the hotel. I have walked this path again and again, I know every damn traffic light along the road, I know where the trees' shadows will be when I come back from my morning swim and I know where they will be when I walk to the bay for my afternoon swim. I know the people living here, I know the visitors who are on vacation. For every tourist that leaves a new one comes. It doesn't seem like it is the end of the season for tourists, only for us swimmers.

My friend Ákos spent a week with me, he was supposed to manage my food from the boat. But no swim means no need for that. Now, he's back in Australia and I'm left as the loneliest man in the world. When I'm awake in Wellington, my family is sleeping. When they're up, it's the middle of the night here.

Some days, I can hear the wind before I open my eyes and I know: not today. Some days, it is quiet. Hope. I open the blinds: storm clouds. The Cook Strait is one of the stormiest straits in the world and just because it's nice in Wellington, it doesn't mean the same thing for the starting point on the South Island. Good swimming days are rare, perfect ones even more so. A good day is not enough for the average long-distance swimmer, but it is for me.

This is what they don't understand.

I've got a real shot at achieving the fastest total Oceans Seven time, I've trained with that damn snorkel, I never skipped a day in the pool. I am prepared. But now, there's somebody ahead of me in the queue who needs a much better day than I would need. The rules of crossing windows are simple: Whoever books first gets to try first. Since I only booked the extra two weeks just now, Dean, who did so a long time ago, has priority. He's a good and mentally strong swimmer, but in conditions like these you must be able to finish in eight hours or the tides will make it impossible. Philip will never let him swim with the conditions being this sketchy.

Another day, another no. I barely practice and spend most of the day lying in bed.

After New Zealand, I would have done the fairly easy

Gibraltar Strait.

I get up to get a glass of water.

I don't know if I'll ever get to swim in Gibraltar.

I sit down in a corner.

I failed at my last swim and my sponsors do not like wasting money.

I stay in the corner for hours.

Nine out of ten people told me to quit after the North Channel. Maybe they were right after all?

I stare at the wall.

Should I just go home?

At around 1 p.m., I call Móni. It's 3 a.m. in Hungary.

With an empty, weak voice, I complain about how alone I feel. How I lost trust in myself. How I don't trust Philip's weather judgement. How out of my control everything is.

Móni listens. When she speaks up, I barely recognize her voice.

"I can hear that you are very down. Now you get up and do it!" she starts. Like a drill sergeant, she goes at me. It works. The very next day, I'm back to training in the ocean. Móni has saved me from across the globe via phone.

Days pass. I move to an even cheaper place. I barely have any money left. A week passes. Sunshine. I show the organizers the weather forecast. They turn me down. "You don't trust us? Okay. Go home and never come back," they tell me.

Whenever there is a small window of opportunity, Dean wants to try – and I understand him. It's a 45-minute drive to the harbor and then a one-hour boat ride to get to the starting point. On Tuesday and Wednesday, they get on their way, but they turn back once they see the conditions around the starting point. Just a good day, not a very good day.

Three days before the end of the window, we have a big meeting.

"Sorry guys, but that's it. The season is over," Philip tells us. I should have expected this, but I still feel like I got kicked in the gut. I spent five weeks in this godforsaken place. For nothing. Dean signs up for next year. "I'm not sure if I can come back," I tell Philip.

Later that night, he calls me.

"There may be a chance. Probably not, but maybe. I'll let you know tomorrow morning."

I have an anxiety-riddled breakfast, waiting for my phone to ring. As I get back to my room at around 8 a.m., Philip finally calls. "It's still not good. But what do you think?" he asks.

"I'll be at your place soon," I say.

Back to this book's prologue: We're on our way across the Strait to the starting point on the South Island. One of the boat's old skippers is a bit grumpy. "On days like this, we usually don't go out," he said when we left.

I should have a two-hour-window in which the conditions on the coast are okay. Not perfect, not even good, but okay. That will have to be enough. By the time the weather turns really bad, I'll be out on the open water. Dean would have been too smart to try in these conditions anyways.

Philip has promised me this one chance before I head home: If I want to swim, he will let me.

I play the professional, but inside, I scream of joy.

The waves toss our boat around like a little toy.

"I never get nauseous on ships," I think to myself as I throw up off the side of the boat.

Once we get to the starting point, Philip looks at me. "So…?"

This must be what Dean saw all those days in the previous weeks. The sea looks much worse than I hoped. But I've flown across the globe. I waited for weeks. I struggled through this boat ride. "I will try," I tell him. One of the old skippers puts his hands on my shoulders and stares into my eyes. "You are a brave man," he says. I'm not sure if he approves of my decision.

Philip gets himself ready. The main boat is too big to

stay close to me when I swim, so he lowers his orange rubber dinghy into the water and jumps in.

No matter how much protective cream I put on my skin, there's always this breathtaking shock when I jump into the freezing water. A jolt of electricity goes through my body, piercing my core and getting stuck there. For a while, it feels as if there's this tension that expands throughout my belly and chest, until I fight it off and get my body moving.

The waves have pushed the ship back, we are closer to the shore than we planned. I need to start off strongly to avoid the rocks and there are far more jellyfish than expected, but they usually hover at around a meter below the surface. As I swim above them, I see their transparent domes, waiting for me to make a careless move. A leg or an arm reaching down too far as I move through the water. Sure, I know jellyfish are not evil creatures plotting to hurt me. But swimming face-first into a Portuguese man o' war will leave you with some hard feelings towards them.

Most swimmers give up at a wind speed of around 15 to 20 knots – about 37 kilometers per hour. I *start* at 20 knots. "It will get worse after around two hours," Philip told me on the boat as the waves threw themselves against its hull. In the water, it sort of feels like I am stuck inside a washing machine. I'm the dirty laundry that gets tossed around jagged rocks and venomous jellyfish.

The freezing slaps of the waves pull me away from the worries of the last five weeks and toss me into reality. I'm a boxer hearing the final notes of his entrance song. This is when it matters.

This is my big fight.

I find my rhythm and make my way through the dangerous, rocky start.

Hours pass.

Long-distance swimming can get monotonous, but this monotony sometimes makes way for some magical things. A few hours after the start, a pod of cheerful dolphins joins me. To swim with them reminds one of how easy swimming is. How fast and effortlessly a living creature can move through water relieves me.

It's just water.

The waves have mostly faded by now. Swim. The dolphins jump out of the water and, in a perfect arch, back into the water. Swim.

I still haven't seen a shark. I prefer it this way.

Every twenty minutes, it is feeding time. Philip hands me my drinks and gels, always on time and exactly the way I like it. I wolf them down as quickly as possible and then: swim. Hours of training in the pool at home have tuned my inner clock quite well, but I still rely on the feeding as my backup stopwatch. It's easy to lose track of time after four hours on the open water. Eat, swim, swim, swim, eat, swim, swim, swim, eat.

Five or six hours must have passed. I can see the finishing line: barren, rocky hills with a few sorry bushes. They could not look more beautiful to me. I must be around two kilometers from the coast, a little more than thirty minutes of swimming at my usual pace.

I'm still feeling strong. My arms pierce the surface of the water like I mean it. Splash, pull, shoulder up, arm out, arm forward, splash. You can tell that you are losing power when the arms merely fall into the water, happily succumbing to gravity. I won't let this happen. This is why I trained with a snorkel for months: less oxygen, more stamina.

The dolphins have left me a while ago. Philip waves me over: feeding time.

Swim.

I'm not getting any closer to the coastline. The hills must still be about 1.5 kilometers away.

Something must be wrong.

I'm not moving forward. The current is too strong. For every meter my arms pull me ahead, the tide drags me back two with a relentless grip.

Futility tires the mind, and when the mind weakens, so does the body.

Swim. Stronger. Faster. Next feeding. I'm not moving.

Philip changes the boat's course to lead me onto a turn to the left. I'm now swimming parallel to the coastline, catching glimpses of those boring hills every time I turn my head to the right to breathe. I don't know what this means, but I know I must trust my pilot. When I am in the water, he is the boss. Him saying "come back next year" seems like it was a long time ago. I know I can trust him; he wants my success as much as I do. And he has the data. I only have my swim trunks, my goggles and the ocean.

Feed. Swim.

I should have touched the rocks on the North Island an hour ago.

The sea is winning. I don't know if I can make it and that thought is the first step towards defeat.

I'm moving my arms, but I'm not making any headway. It's like wanting to run away from something in a nightmare, but no matter what I do, the monster chasing me comes closer and closer.

We are turning towards the shore again.

I must have swum three or four kilometers along the coastline, I can now feel that the tide is weaker. I can progress: splash, pull, shoulder up, arm out, splash. Second wind, they call it. Splash, splash, splash.

I see the hills coming closer. New Zealand's North Island, its beauty almost as renowned as the South Island's, is reaching out to me, extending a delicate hand. I just need to grab it.

If only I could see what's in the water.

This hand I'm about to grab has jagged nails. In order to finish, I must touch the rocky coast, but there is a myriad of rocks and crags with razor-sharp edges in the water before it. As if the jellyfish from the start had turned to stone, now hunting for blood instead of mere pain.

I must swim slowly, controlled.

Some last, exhausted splashes. I reach out.

Finish.

A wave catches me from behind.

I'm being carried towards the rock, but my exhausted arms manage to save me. I push myself off.

I have won the battle.

There's a messy storm of emotions inside me. The feeling is only there for a few seconds before the pain comes, but these few seconds are unbelievable. Nothing can match its intensity.

This is what I live for. Life is about being happy and I find happiness in moments like these.

A giant wave crashes into me, but I'm far enough from the rocks not to get hurt.

I hear shouts from the boat. I know that Philip is glad that he trusted me.

I think about Móni and the girls. How proud they will be. I climb onto the boat and scream of joy.

Number five: complete.

TWO TO GO

May 2017, Hungary

The first few weeks at home after a successful Oceans Seven swim are pure stress. This time, it's even more hectic because Móni got us two small dogs while I was gone. The other stuff is the same as always: a radio interview here, a newspaper feature there, a TV appearance to top it off – and again, and again, and again. For a country of ten million people, Hungary has a surprisingly high number of broadcasting stations. I appreciate every single one of them – and so do my sponsors.

It's funny. When my North Channel swim ended in the hospital, I had swum 26.4 kilometers in seven hours and four minutes. I was a loser. Now, I swam 26 kilometers in six hours and 57 minutes. Depending on the conditions, those extra 400 meters would have taken me about five or six minutes. But now, I am a winner. Everybody wants to talk to me, shake my hand, take a selfie.

They treat me like a war hero now. They should have done so last year. I crossed my limits and that got me close to dying – isn't that what war heroes do?

But I love my country. Just like I have learned to accept the mysterious ways the waves and the currents work, I have learned to accept how things work here. The media wants you when you succeed.

CHILDHOOD MEMORIES: BUDAPEST

1990, Budapest

Attila was alone. Not in a bad sense – one of his swimming buddies from Zalaegerszeg had been taken in by his new club too so he wasn't lonely. But nobody told him what to do. He had to go to training and beat his target times. But away from the pool? Nobody cared.

Attila was free.

He didn't have to fear going back home. No more worrying whether he'd done something wrong.

Even though he was still just 16 years old, he tried to spend as little time in Zalaegerszeg as possible: About three times a year, Attila returned for a day. He missed his mom and he knew she missed him too – and for that, he felt sorry – but his fear and discomfort were just too much whenever he was back home.

His routine in Budapest was simple: Wake up, breakfast, training. They made the kids swim faster, longer and more often than Attila was used to at home. He could feel himself getting faster and faster. He was in the elite group with four other boys and they were pushing each other during every training session. When he beat the others, he'd mock them just as much as they did it to him when they won. They all knew that if somebody slowed down, there would be plenty of kids waiting to take their spots.

MONEY

Fall 2017, Hungary

I remember the smelly hotel rooms back from when I started. I always will.

When my Oceans Seven mission began, I had little money. The English Channel and Tsugaru are expensive and I had fewer sponsors back then. I don't live in luxury now, but I am a little flusher. I spent three times as much on my swim in New Zealand as I did when I crossed the English Channel.

During the last World Cup years, I had worked at a small family business, doing lots of different things on the side to earn some cash. But you can't compete like I did with a normal 9-to-5 job. Nobody lets you just leave for two or three months every year.

Once you switch to doing the Oceans Seven, that changes. Most of the others just work a regular job and spend their holidays completing big swims. But if you have a normal day job in Hungary, you don't earn enough money to pay the fees, boats, flight tickets and accommodation. I had to go all in on my training and find a way to make a living with the help of sponsors. I'm one of very, very few professional swimmers aiming to complete the Oceans Seven.

But once you're in the ocean, money doesn't matter. You finish – or you don't. Nature, the elements… they don't care about bills.

GIBRALTAR

October/November 2017, Spain

Beating the record time in Gibraltar is impossible for me. It's such a short swim that for swimmers used to doing 10-kilometer races in the pool, it's a piece of cake. But I still need to think of my overall time, so I aim to set one of the best times of this season.

Things in Spain are relaxed. I still had to send a lot of documents – filled out forms, medical stuff – but in general, the organizers aren't really giving me a reason to stress out. "Mañana, mañana," they say. "Tomorrow, tomorrow."

Before I left home, I had asked if there were any other swimmers during my set time window who I would be able to train with. The event's organizer, Laura, told me: Yes, a Brazilian guy named Aldo. I can tell that she is struggling to keep up with all the bureaucracy and I can't blame her – her father Rafa died of cancer two months ago. He used to run the business.

When I show up, Aldo is there already. A few days later, Zach, an American, arrives. I mostly train with him. I keep it relaxed, just roll my arms, keep everything nice and fluid. Zach is always ahead of me.

I often ask him how he feels after training.

"Very relaxed," he says.

I wished I could feel relaxed at that fast pace he's always going.

In a normal year, everybody swims Gibraltar on their own. Only this season, they had to cancel so many swims that they put most people together in groups. Laura tells me that I may have to swim with Zach. "I'll think about it," I tell her.

My window is from October 26 to November 4. It's very late in the season, but swimming the Cook Strait took priority when I did my planning. As always, I check the weather data on three different platforms and it doesn't look good.

"Maybe you can swim on Monday," Laura tells me.

"Monday doesn't look good to me," I tell her. "Next weekend, it should be fine."

"But that won't work for you," she says.

"Why? Saturday is August 4."

"Yes. You booked your window until the second," Laura tells me.

"What?"

"Didn't you read the email?"

"What email?" I ask. "Show me."

She can't find it. "We changed your window, now it's from October 23 to Thursday."

I feel so stupid. Nobody told me about this when I kept sending my documents referring to the window from October 26 to November 4. Laura is trying her best, but this probably got lost somewhere when she had to take over the business from Rafa.

"If not Monday, maybe Thursday will work. We'll see," she says. "Mañana."

My brain starts whirling. Can I swim? What if I can't? I have already been successful this year, but I want to check Gibraltar off the list. The season here is supposed to be over already, usually the last swims are around mid-October. It's so windy here that it's a kite-surfer's paradise.

Monday comes. "We can't go today. Mañana," Laura says.

Zach calls me. After some small talk, he asks: "What do you think about our speed?"

I can see where this is going.

"I think maybe we are similar," I tell him.

"Yes, maybe," he says. "What if the conditions stay bad? Can we swim together if there's no other way?"

I don't like swimming with somebody else, especially considering he has been much faster than me during our training sessions. A group must stay close together, so you need lots of luck to have the same rhythm as your teammates. But I want this swim off the list.

"Yes, we can try," I say. At this point, I'm more worried that we won't even get a chance at all. According to my calculations, Thursday doesn't work. It's getting colder by the day.

On Wednesday, the organizers call us in for a technical meeting. Laura explains the rules, the wind, the currents. Whenever she talks about our speed, she says that it looks like I'm faster. "Do you agree to swim with Zach?" she asks. I tell her yes, so we plan for a group swim on Thursday.

After the meeting, Zach comes up to me. "Why does she think I'm not fast?" he asks.

"I don't know," I reply. I really don't. "She knows my results, my awards...," I try to explain. But I have seen Zach in training. He may have to slow down for me.

Wednesday evening, my phone rings.

"6.30 mañana, we meet at the harbor."

Mañana! I get to swim!

I sleep well, everybody is on time and we leave for the starting point. The conditions look fine.

"If it stays this nice, I'll do it around three hours. If the conditions are really good and I can push it, it'll be less than three hours. If things turn bad, around four hours," I tell Zach.

He seems surprised. "Oh, for me, 3 hours 30 minutes is okay," he says.

Now I am the surprised one. From what I've seen in the last few days, he will surely be faster.

I spend a few minutes by myself as the crew gets the boat ready. It should be a cakewalk, but I feel uneasy. As we leave the harbor, I tell Laura: "I'm 44. He's 26. He always was a little faster than me during our swims here."

"So?"

"We have to stick together, those are the rules. I'm worried about not being able to keep up with him and him having to wait."

At least I have no reason to be worried whether I'll make it to the other side. As we get to the starting point, I say goodbye to my friends. The escort boat is tiny, it only fits the pilot and one more person – and that will be Chris, Zach's friend.

It'll just be a quick tour. Jump in, wait for the starting sign, swim.

Zach swims ahead, I follow.

He's even faster than I feared. I try to stay close to him.

I never had to start this fast. Not even at the Tsugaru Strait, when I was in perfect shape.

I do my best to keep up. Strong, fast strokes, strong kicks, focus on the perfect body position.

There's no way I can keep up with him for long.

I do my best. I don't want to mess up his swim and look bad.

Strokestrokebreathstrokestrokebreathstrokestrokebreat
h. I inhale much harder than usual to get in the air I need.
I haven't had a race like this since my World Cup times.

Zach slows down. The past 20 minutes have been pure suffering, but I can finally keep up with him swimming my normal pace. It's a relief – physically and mentally. I can't be sure that he won't speed up again, but for now, I don't have to worry about making him wait.

Minute by minute, I pay less attention to him.

Finally, I fall into the perfect rhythm. This is exactly how I want it to be.

Zach fixes his goggles. I slow down and wait for him to catch up.

When he reaches me, I speed up again.

He doesn't.

"Dude, swim. Swim!" I want to shout.

He moves so slowly, I can barely stay next to him without treading water.

I feel like a kid during the last few minutes of a long school day, the whole body itching to go out and run and play and burn off all that excess energy. Zach doesn't seem to feel that way. He stops to fix the goggles again, breaking our rhythm a second time. He catches up and says, "Okay, go".

I am swimming ahead now, not as fast as I want to, but at a reasonable pace. Now that his goggles are fixed, he will surely pass me soon.

Surely, he will.

Surely, he will?

I don't know what that start was about, but now I realize I am faster.

At least my worries of not being able to keep up with him were unfounded.

We make it to our first feeding. Chris gives us our drinks from the Zodiac, our supply boat. At least he's doing a good job. I finish my drink and look over to Zach.

He hasn't even started his drink.

I know I'm an unusually fast drinker – I always warn the crew before a swim that I do not want to chat and that I'm just going to wolf down my drink – but this is just ridiculous.

We're not having a romantic dinner at a restaurant, we are trying to swim across the Mediterranean Sea! Every second spent drinking and eating is a lost one.

Zach and I could hardly be a worse match. I breathe to my right side, he breathes to his left side. Because the one guy we could bring onto the boat is his friend, we swim to the right of the boat. That sucks. Swimmers always need to see the boat – not just for psychological reasons, but also to make sure you're actually going in the right direction. Swimming a straight line without any reference points is hard enough in open water, but there's always a chance the boat changes course. Now, only Zach gets to see the boat when he turns his head to breathe – all I see is him. I must trust that he's swimming parallel to the boat. But we keep drifting away.

So.

Slow.

And he is getting even slower.

It feels like I'm stuck in a slow-motion replay. What my arms are doing doesn't even resemble rhythmic swimming anymore. After our second feeding, I decide to change two things: First, I now turn to both sides to breathe – it's not like I could be losing any valuable pace and this way, I can see the boat. Second, I change my rhythm. I swim at a proper pace for a short while and then stop to wait.

Some people are happy to finish a swim without being exhausted. "It was easy," they'll then say.

But that's not me.

When I'm in the water, I'm reaping the fruits of my labor all those months before. The days spent in Algeciras before the swim, the weeks I spent organizing the trip, the endless hours I spent training in the pool. Everything for those few hours of swimming.

I want to make them count.

But I won't say anything. Not a word. Inside, I am screaming: "We are slow!" But I won't open my mouth. It's painfully frustrating not to release any of the anger, but in another way, it's liberating to know that it just is not an option. It wouldn't change anything. Accept it, move on.

We get to our next feeding. I'm done within a few seconds, he slowly finishes his food, I say "okay", and we continue.

Swimming this slowly leaves a lot of room for thinking.

Three hours of training a day would've been enough for this.

That's four hours per day I could've spent with my family.

I didn't expect that my biggest challenge at any Oceans Seven swim would be having to wait, but the prime goal still is arriving at shore.

At every feeding, I boil up again inside.

But I swim. And wait.

Besides our pace, it goes quite well. The conditions are perfect after all.

At the technical meeting, we were told that if the final stretch looks safe, we can each swim our own pace. As I see the Moroccan shore coming closer, I ask our pilot Fernando: "Can I move? Can I move?"

"No. Stay here."

I can feel my blood boiling. I can't help but go a little faster and Zach immediately falls behind.

Fernando turns the boat and tells me to wait.

I feel imaginary steam coming out of my pores.

About 200 meters away from the coast, I try again. As I talk to Fernando, Zach passes me and speeds up. Full speed, fast rhythm, strong kicks. Like it's a damn competition.

It's a race now.

I catch up to Zach and swim next to him for a few strokes.

Now he knows that it's a race, too.

I keep swimming my normal pace and he quickly falls behind. As I touch the rocks, he's behind me by about 50 meters.

When he climbs out on the rocks, I swim over to

congratulate him.

"How was your swim?" I ask.

"Oh, it was easy."

He can't be serious.

Unlike me, at least he looks like a swimmer that gave his all. His gas tank seems to be empty. Myself…I've been more exhausted after some of my training sessions. "You don't look like you swam from Europe to Africa," the head captain tells me when we get back to the boat.

I don't feel like it either. That's what makes everything so frustrating.

At 1 p.m., I'm back at the restaurant with my friends having lunch. Like I had just left for a morning training swim.

Something is missing from the experience, but I've completed Oceans Seven swim number six.

And in the end, that's all that matters. Well, that and the Oceans Seven overall record. And I'm still on track for that.

CHILDHOOD MEMORIES:
MÓNI

October 1980, Zalaegerszeg

There she was.

Attila's heart beat faster. Du-dumm, dum-dumm, dumdumdum. Thank God his friends didn't notice. Móni was the prettiest girl he had ever seen. The two had talked a few times after school and it was really hard for Attila to act normal around her. God, she was so pretty, and he thought she liked him. He liked her for sure. But she was a girl! What would his friends say?

She had seen him. That smile! Attila's heart jumped up and down and forward and out. How was he supposed to stay calm with this girl smiling at him? He knew that she saw what her smile was doing to him. She knew that he knew and he knew that she knew that he knew and she knew that he knew that she knew that he knew and she still smiled. But he didn't know what was happening to him.

"Hi, Attila."

"Hi, Móni."

She smiled. He could only stare at her. It took her a while to say something.

"Do you want to go play in the park after school?"

EMERGENCY. Attila's brain plunged into chaos. There were a hundred words jumping to his head and none of them made sense.

"Answer her!" he silently screamed to himself.

"Ummmmm…yes."

She smiled. "Okay, see you then!"

Smiling and waving her goodbye is all he managed.

MÓNI AND THE KIDS

2017, Hungary

I'm on my way to the airport. For once, it's not because I'm flying somewhere.

Móni's schedules and mine have been so complicated that I need to meet her at the airport to spend a little time with her. I'm arriving from a meeting in Zalaegerszeg, she is leaving for work. We'll have five, maybe ten minutes. But those are the things we need to do to see each other.

As I'm passing the drivers that obey the speed limit, I smile. I just love how right this feels. I know how ridiculous it must be to normal people…it feels ridiculous to me, too. But five minutes are five minutes.

I like driving to see her. The six-year-old Attila still lives inside me and remembers waiting for school to end so he could see her.

Not much has changed, I just have a driving license and pay taxes now.

I often think of how lucky I am to be with Móni. Without that one random meeting, my life would have gone in such a different direction. Months after we got together, she told me something about that day we met at Starbucks. For years, she had ordered her coffee to take-away. That day was the first time she decided to sit down.

When I was worrying about my window closing when I was in New Zealand, we talked on the phone every day. Even if it was 2 a.m. at home – she never refused to talk to me. She never complained that she was tired. She never made me feel like I was bothering her. She always understood me. Having somebody who loves and supports you is one of the best things one can have in life.

Móni is perfect for me in so many ways. And so are her daughters.

A long time ago, I decided that I would never have children myself. I have the same genes as my father. What if I would be like him?

I didn't want anyone to go through the things I had to endure in my own childhood.

With the girls, it's different. I'm not their biological father, so I don't act in the ways that I feared I would.

Once, they put my patience to the test.

It won't surprise anybody that young girls are into Disney princesses. But the number of different princesses will surprise anyone who is not blessed with a daughter or niece.

One afternoon, the twins want to play a game.

They show me a princess doll and I have to guess her name. If my guess is wrong, I must do some exercise they come up with on the spot and they tell me the name. The game goes on until I have gotten all the names right.

The first princess is blonde. I can't even think of a name to say. And off I go, jumping through the whole house on my right foot.

The second one is easy. Everyone knows Ariel, the little mermaid.

The third one…sort of looks Chinese? I have no clue. Ten pushups it is.

It's a long afternoon. I keep failing, Móni keeps feeding them suggestions for what they could make me do. One of the girls just started ballet classes…let's just say I'm glad there's no video footage of my attempts at being a ballerina.

Cinderella, Jasmin (second try), Elsa (I swear to God, I can hear that Frozen song when I see the doll), Rapunzel, Snow White (first try), Belle, Tiana, Mulan (who actually IS Chinese), Anna (one Frozen princess just isn't enough, I guess), Ariel, Tiana, Elsa again (*LET IT GOOOOOO*).

Aaaah, family.

ACCLIMATIZING

Winter/Spring 2018, USA

Almost dying has a big upside: It's very easy to learn from it.

I won't be overwhelmed by the cold again. Acclimatization is my main priority this time, I will train in the cold as much as I can afford to. Sadly, that won't be too much as I lost a lot of sponsoring money. It's terrible timing in the year my most important swim takes place, but an important sponsor needs to save money and I'm one of the victims of the budget cut. It completely messes up my finances. When they inform me, I cancel my reservations for San Francisco and Ireland and book something cheaper. It feels like I'm back in the old days.

I must cut back on the competitions I go to as part of my preparation, down to…one. In spring, all the competitions in Europe are either too short or too cold, so I will have to go overseas. I decide to keep the S.C.A.R. series in Arizona, because I can stay at the house of Steven Minaglia's friend. I fly there via San Francisco, where I can swim in the cold waters around Alcatraz.

To make up for the lack of competitions, I'll just have to train a lot more and harder in the pool.

And that I do, always with my goal in mind. The final swim, the final triumph. No excuses. Nikos would be proud.

As I arrive to the US, I am anxious to see how well I will do. Training in the pool is important, foundational, indispensable, yadda yadda yadda. But competitions show you how well your body really works. In training, when you're suffering through your program to optimize your development, you swim different intervals with fixed rest times. When you push yourself for eight hours straight, that's when your body shows its true colors.

As I'm getting ready to swim in San Francisco, I get a text from Móni. The boiler at home isn't working.

Sometimes, we can fix these issues together over the phone. Sometimes, I can't do anything.

Moments like these make me feel terrible. Móni has a partner – but sometimes, she doesn't.

My swims in San Francisco and at the S.C.A.R. series are not perfect, but good enough. My body gets used to cold water, and that's what this was about.

For the two final steps of my acclimatization, I head back to Europe: At the end of May, I join the *HITtheWALL* training camp in Ireland. It is run by Infinity, the company I will swim with in the summer. At the camp, I get to know my organizer, Padraig, better and spend lots of time with the whole Infinity crew. The camp ends with a six-and-a-half-hour swim that counts as qualification for the North Channel crossing. That channel is so brutal that not everyone can just give it a try.

After a month in Hungary, I fly back for the Cork Distance Week – the one single thing I'm not changing in my preparations. It may not have been enough back in 2016, but nobody can prepare you better for a cold swim than the legend Ned Denison. "You're very different from two years ago. You're ready now," he tells me.

If he says so, I will be an Oceans Seven finisher soon.

NORTH CHANNEL II

July/August 2018, Northern Ireland

"This is the best summer in a long, long time. We've had nine weeks of sunshine; I can't believe it. We've never seen that," a British lady tells me. The bad news: The historic heatwave ends the week before my swim. For six weeks, it hadn't rained. Now, it's been nothing but rain for three straight days. A friend of mine is staying in a bed-and-breakfast and today, his host told him that she had to turn on the heating for the first time since May. It's almost August! Somewhere, the devil himself is messing with the weather controls, trying to screw me over.

I stay in Newtownards. This small town slowly drives me insane. Two journalists from a Hungarian TV channel have joined me to film a documentary about my final swim, so besides my trainings, I am busy giving interviews in different shooting spots.

Oh, and I'm out of money.

There are some issues with the receipts I handed in for sponsorships. They require the bills to have my name and the full name of my swimming club, and not every accommodation managed to put that on their receipts. I will hopefully manage to take care of all that when I'm back in Hungary, but for now I'm out thousands of Euros – or rather British Pounds.

I save money wherever I can, so when I go to buy a new drinking bottle, I grab the cheapest one. I can handle drinking from an impractical bottle and eating the cheapest cookies. But I know that if anything unexpected comes up, I can't pay for it. That feeling weighs on me like a heavy rock.

None of the other swimmers have to deal with this. I've gotten used to constantly drawing the shortest straw, but it hurts a lot more in the week before the biggest swim of my life.

At least Ion is with me now. He's a wide-shouldered giant with a booming voice and all the open water experience anybody could need. Ion completed the Oceans Seven this year. He was born in Moldova, but has been living in Ireland for decades, so he sounds very Irish.

Ion knows the North Channel. He is the kind of guy that says sentences like "This is no micky mouse swim", "For this, you need *cojones* like an elephant", or "You don't want the water to be flat...then all the jellies come up and say hi to Johnny!"

It took Ion over 16 hours to cross the North Channel. I couldn't imagine staying in that icy water for that long. For the Oceans Seven overall record, I need to finish in 12 hours and ten minutes. The North Channel record still stands at nine hours and 35 minutes. Both are possible.

Every day, three other channel swimmers and I go to Donaghadee to train with a lovely local swimming group called the Chunky Dunkers. Some of them could be my grandparents, but they go for a swim every day of the year! They're all very cordial and supportive people, but it's wasted on me. As I get out of the car, I think about my empty bank account. I change, I think about old receipts, I put on my goggles, I think about the trivialities that keep the money away from me. I look at the others preparing, I think of how none of them have these worries. I leave my swim cap in the car, I...I don't even think anymore. Only worries, spiced with some anger.

The swim cap stays in the car for a reason. I will try to swim without it for the first time here, to shock my head and harden it for the long swim.

The four of us who will swim the channel split from the group. I am the strongest of us, but it's still good to train with other guys with the same ambitions. There's an Indian guy training with us. He's 19. 19! I think he will have a hard time. He is in great shape and training hard, but experience is crucial here.

The Chunky Dunkers swim a small lap while the four of us go all the way to the lighthouse across the bay. As we swim, my head jumps between swimming and worrying.

Donaghadee has the classic beachfront you find in most British coastal towns: Every house has a different color, most in pastel tones, some in strong blues and greens. I would love to keep admiring it, but the water is around twelve degrees. The conditions are still nicer than they were during the last few training days, the sun peeks through here and there and the wind is a refreshing breeze instead of an icy storm.

It has always been a little painful to see how easy some swimmers have it, especially those that put much less effort into it. I don't blame them – most of them work a normal job after all. But they still get to do three swims a year while I need to fight to afford even two a season. That's why I focus so much on being the fastest overall – here, people won't pass me just because they have more money.

When I started this journey, only two people had completed the Oceans Seven. Last year, that number was six – and by now, five more have made it. I can see the peak of the mountain, but some unfair power forces me to wait at the last camp while others pass me.

When I touch the coast of Scotland, none of this will matter anymore.

As is often the case in areas with complicated weather, there is a lot of back and forth regarding possible starting times. "We'll have to wait a few more days," I'm told, just for the weather to improve shortly after. "Friday night, you can swim," they tell me on Thursday.

As things change, I must accept them. I prepare my stuff

and lie down a little before I head to the harbor.

I'm used to not sleeping much before a swim, but there is one problem: I didn't manage to go to the toilet before we left. My stomach needs to be mostly empty to feel comfortable while swimming. It's a little awkward to tell this to the TV crew before we board the boat, but I do it. It's not all glamour in the swimming business. At least I leave out the part how I will......finish the digestion process during the swim. It won't be the first time.

The water, as always: same same but different. On the way to the starting point, we speed across a black, glossy surface, shimmering like polished mud. The half moon is partly hidden by clouds. It's been eight days since the longest lunar eclipse of the century.

I go through the feeding plan with Ion once more. Usually he's a true jokester, but now he's all serious. It's only a short ride to the starting point and I barely notice the others chatting and taking photos. Ion finishes putting the anti-chafing cream on me and I keep watching the water.

It is amazingly still. I could not have asked for calmer conditions.

Still, I know there are no safe bets in this channel.

My goal time for the total Oceans Seven record is 12:10 hours. That...well, I'll make it if I finish at all.

"Time to get ready," I hear. I can see the lights on the shore guiding me to the starting point.

I fix a flashing light to my swim cap, give a thumbs up for one last photo and jump into the water.

It feels good. Not too cold, the surface calm like water in a pool. I get to the shore. Lots of locals have showed up to cheer me on despite it being the middle of the night. As always, the rule is: Stand up, wave and start swimming.

I try to get into a good rhythm right away. Stroke, paddle, stroke, paddle.

Jellyfish. The pain is intense. Next Jellyfish.

How unlucky could I be? I'm not even back to where the escort boat is waiting and I'm already collecting jellies as if I was working on a scrapbook of pain.

Most of the jellies here are lion's mane jellyfish – no man o' wars, but not much more fun, either.

Stroke, paddle, stroke, paddle. Block out the pain.

I get back to the escort boat and try to refocus on my swim.

My body is strong. As long as the sea stays the way it is now, I'll be fine.

Thanks to the good conditions, I can stay quite close to the boat, so I lose less time during the feedings. I drink my sports drink and eat power gels every 30 minutes. At every other feeding I get an extra Oreo cookie.

As daylight arrives, I start to see the armies of jellyfish gathered just below the surface. After two hours of swimming, I have touched more than I did in my whole crossing attempt two years ago. I remember Ion saying "You don't want the water to be flat...then all the jellies come up and say hi to Johnny!"

Oh, how flat it is.

But I'm okay. Just some discomfort in my stomach and some spikes of pain here and there, but my arms, legs and mind are fine. And it's them that carry me to Scotland.

Swim.

I feel bloated as I haven't managed to pee yet.

Another jelly. The pain is brutal.

Another hour passes. Something has changed.

As if I was wearing clothes that are one size too small, I feel that the range of my movements is being held back by something. It's not the cold; I'm fine with that and the sun is helping.

Swim. Feed. Swim.

The feeling is getting worse.

My breathing weakens. It's as if I was wearing a snorkel again, only that I haven't gotten used to the restricted airflow. My body lacks the power to properly get air into my system.

I don't even feel tired.

I try to pee. I can't. At the feeding, I see how much body control I have lost. I can barely speak and I spill half of my drink into the sea.

Swim. I can't see the coast yet, but I know that my pace was great in the beginning. It shouldn't be too far.

It's a fight. But I guess it would have been boring without a fight. I'm on full autopilot now, so I don't even try to dodge jellies when somebody from the boat shouts for me to swim around them.

I've hit so many, it doesn't matter anymore.

I'm slow, but I keep moving. This is as fast as I can be with my muscles being so limp.

Jelly. Pain. Swim. My stomach. I'm so full. Swim. I'm worried. So slow. Swim. Take a break. Swim. Try to pee. No. Swim.

This is what I trained for.

Time for my next feeding. I've been in the water for six hours. I see Ion and the crew shout something, but I don't hear it. I think that I shout "It feels bad" in their direction.

I get my food, turn away from the boat and swim.

I see a star.

It's growing.

Black.

Somebody is with me.

It's dry around me.

Slowly.

I hear voices.

I don't understand.

I'll sleep.

I'm not alone here.

I'm not in the water.

I'm in a bed.

I'll sleep for a bit.

I'm still here.

Móni is here.

I hear voices. Móni is still here.

She smiles. I see worry and relief on her face.

Something sticky is on my face and tubes are coming out of my body. I feel weird.

Móni starts talking to me. "What is the last thing you remember?" she asks.

"A feeding," I answer.

"Do you know how many hours you swam?" she asks.

"Something like six."

"Ten and a half."

"What?"

"Yes. Ten and a half."

I close my eyes. I am exhausted.

"Do you remember how close the coast was?" Móni asks.

"No. I couldn't see it."

"You almost made it."

Almost. Damn.

I spend my next few days putting together what happened through conversations with Móni, Ion and the amazing personnel at the Ulster hospital.

I swam for four more hours than I can now remember, but I was in a terrible shape. As the current was in my favor during that part of the swim, I was still making progress towards the coast. The crew was hoping I would finish, but when I didn't respond to their shouts anymore, they had to pull me out. Before that, Ion had apparently been swimming next to me for an hour. I was semi-conscious for a while on the boat, but only responded to things said in Hungarian. The crew covered me in every jacket and coat they could find and took me back to the port in Bangor. There, I was picked up by an ambulance. My core temperature at that time was 28.6 degrees Celsius. I was taken to Ulster hospital, where I talked to doctors. I remember none of that. It took two teams of doctors working non-stop for hours to save my life.

The jellyfish toxins had first made me incapable of

peeing, which set off a cascade of disastrous consequences, each one crippling me a little more. My digestion system stopped working, so the food stayed in the stomach. None of it could be metabolized to fuel the muscles. The kidneys stopped working, which allowed the jellyfish venom to stay in my body. My muscles weakened, so my body temperature sunk dramatically. All of this put together, combined with a body and mind trained to swim on autopilot no matter what... Well, that's what you need to almost die.

The chief doctor treating me, Bob Darling, told me that my oxygen saturation was around 30 percent. At around 80 percent, organs start failing; at 30 percent, the brain is usually considered dead. My left lung had fully collapsed. I had swallowed dangerous amounts of sea water, so the right lung was in danger too. Dr. Darling didn't believe I would make it through the night.

They put me in an artificial coma for a day.

"Attila is a very fit and active man, who is very strong and able to sustain severe conditions in a resilient fashion and he was able to survive this life-threatening event," Dr. Darling is being quoted by the BBC. "Attila, you got lucky," is what I read into that.

After Móni goes back to Hungary, Padraig and Jacqui keep visiting me every day. They bring me everything I need, but mostly we talk, talk, and talk. About life, about death, about goals, about doubts and about persistence. With every conversation we have, our connection grows.

Days after they wake me up from the artificial coma, I still have a tube going down my throat to help me breathe. The toxins are still clogging my system. Eight days after my swim, I go to the toilet for the first time.

GOING HOME

August 2018, Ulster Hospital

In the United Kingdom, murder by poison was considered one of the ultimate crimes – High Treason – for a while. The "Poisoning Act 1530" stipulates that perpetrators were to be boiled to death instead of being executed in a more humane way.

Now, I understand why. The jellyfish venom slowly creeps up on you. You can try to fight it mentally, but you can't win. It's evil.

People ask me if this experience changes something, whether I will stop swimming.

Only people who don't know me ask that.

Again, I have proved that I can go to my limits. Wrong time, wrong place. Next year: better time, same place.

I get to leave the hospital on August 14, ten days after I got there. The doctors tell me that I'm not allowed to fly for a while. "If Padraig can't do it, I'll drive you down to Budapest," Jacqui tells me. This is the kind of person she is. Both her and Padraig have visited me every single day I've been here.

I don't want anybody to drive three-thousand kilometers because of me, so we agree that Padraig will take the ferry to England with me and drive me down to London. When I hug him at St Pancras Station, I say goodbye to one of the few people I truly see eye-to-eye with.

From London, I take the train to Brussels, where I get on a different train to Frankfurt and from there, I head to

Vienna. There, Móni picks me up by car.

It feels good. Time to relax. Time to celebrate my new, second birthday.

Balaton, I can't wait for you. Family, holiday, life.

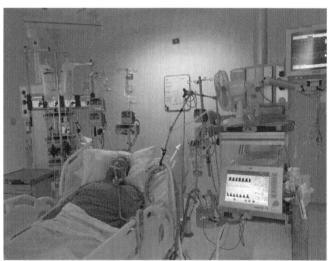

In the hospital.

RETURNING TO THE WATER

October 2018, Santorini

Santorini really is a pretty place. The first flight of my new life, the first swim of my new life. I'm here for the Santorini Experience, a 2.4-kilometer (1.5-mile) swim mostly marketed towards hobby swimmers. I don't mind. I'm not here for a tough race, I'm here to enjoy it. Even better: I'm here to enjoy it with Móni and the kids. During a boat tour two days before the race, I do my first strokes since those fateful ones that I don't remember anymore.

It's still the same.

Water is wet, I feel good.

The sea is still my friend, my home.

The swim takes place on a Sunday. As is always the case in Greece, the sun is shining. It is one of the most beautiful settings in the world. Santorini is an island shaped like a crescent, in the sea off its central coast sits a volcano that's been dormant for millennia. We will start there, swim a little and finish at the old port of the island. There are some swimmers from the Greek national team and a guy from Serbia who will race each other for first place. I won't bother with that.

I'll just feel the water and...yes, have a little taste of competition. I want to be reasonably fast. A man has his principles.

The procedure is nicely simple: Get your number, put it on, get to the boat assigned to your number. I'm number 51, so I join about seventy other swimmers on the first boat to the volcano. The mood at the Old Port is good. Not too many people, not too hectic, hardly any nervous swimmers, just some people happy to be where they are on a Sunday morning. Behind the port, the cliffs rise steeply, all the way to the city of Fira. I took the cable car down, those who decide to walk down the 500 steps arrive sweaty. Móni and the girls are not with me yet, they stayed in bed a bit longer.

As the boat leaves the port, they play "We Are The Champions". A little premature for my taste, but that's the spirit here. Competing is winning. The sun finally rising over the cliffs makes for picturesque scenery.

The volcano is not really what most people would think of when they hear volcano. It's not a big mountain with a nice tip like Mount Fuji, and it's not massive like Mount Etna, either. It's only the peak of the submarined remains of a once-erupted volcano, so it's rather flat, but considerably wide. There, we'll start at a small beach and swim out to the main island.

We get ready while we're waiting for the other boats to arrive. Only pros are allowed to swim without an orange safety buoy attached to their waist, so it's easy to see how few of us pro swimmers there are in a sea of orange dots.

Start. Finally, I am back where I belong.

The sea is moving a little, the waves have small white caps.

Swimming properly is harder than it used to be. My body feels heavy, like I don't get enough oxygen. I don't care about my pace, so I go slow. I don't need to suffer right now.

It's great to swim again.

At the finish, I climb up a ladder to get out onto the pier. As soon as I take the last step, I see Móni and the girls, watching me from the first row right behind the finish.

What a feeling. It's so good to have somebody waiting for you.

I immediately walk over to them and almost forget to take my finishing medal and pose for a few photos.

Afterwards, I take them over to the swimmers' area and talk, and talk, and talk. The girls are so proud, and so is Móni, and so am I, and I want it to be like this forever.

After the swim, I finally get to spend time with Nikos. He is a big man, literally and figuratively. The athletes he's trained have won medals at World and European championships and Olympic Games, but his success is not what makes him so special. Nikos tells me that he is "coaching" his four kids – and that says everything. He approaches coaching as a form of guidance through life. He subtly points you in the right direction when he thinks you need it and he does it more bluntly when the subtle way doesn't work. He says what needs to be said for you to understand. No more, no less.

Nikos sports a full beard with a few grey streaks, his booming voice fills any room. But to me, it's his eyes that define him. Nikos has such a strong gaze. When he looks at you, you know he means it.

A good coach is a busy man. Nikos' phone is constantly ringing because his past and present swimmers ask him for advice on anything. One guy will call him to discuss his breakup, the next call may be about a breaststroke technique that another swimmer has seen somewhere.

My connection to him is irreplaceable despite us not training together, and I'm glad for every meeting we get in person.

FAMILY

Winter 2019, Hungary

My father lives in a different world. You cannot tell a blind man how beautiful the sunset is.

When you open the door to his place, you never know what you'll see. He's… not exactly anti-alcohol. Of course, in his world, he has never been drunk.

When somebody asks him about me, he tells them that he is proud. When we are together at the market in Zalaegerszeg, he boasts about me. "Yes, this is my son!" But when the doors are closed, I hear the same old stories: I'm stupid, I mess everything up, I'm not worth anything.

When my mom was still alive, they never came to any of the galas where I was honored. Mom would've loved to, but she couldn't go alone as she didn't have a driver's license – and she didn't want to go with Dad. He just doesn't know what he can and cannot say to people. Mom always wanted to avoid me getting in trouble for something Dad might say to somebody important – so they decided to stay away.

My brother takes after Dad a bit, so his life is different from mine. The things that are important to him are the things I don't care about and it's the same the other way around. He's 45 years old and lives with his dogs.

When I get back from a swim, I explain the banalities about my experiences to him and Dad: "It was long, I was tired, but it was okay. I felt powerful."

I'm sure that our differences started during our childhood. My brother was a swimmer too, but only for a few years. He then took up running, but without any serious results. He quit sports after elementary school.

While I was hopping from one friend's place to the next, he preferred to stay at home.

He often calls me and it feels like he just wants to talk. "How are you?", "What are you doing?", he asks. I don't know what he really wants. Maybe he feels like it's necessary because we are family, but whenever we talk, I can feel the vast distance between us as if it was floating in front of me like those slow mosquitoes in the summertime. I'm just not the kind of person to call someone without a reason. I'll reply to one of his "questions" and then, there's a few seconds of "uhm, uhm, uhm…" – and then: "What is the weather like?"

Everybody in our extended family says that we're completely different. I'm like my mother used to be.

Ever since I lost her, I feel like I put more and more distance between my family and myself. When she was alive, we were always somehow connected.

I get jealous whenever I see Móni's family. They are what it's supposed to be like. Seeing her parents makes me realize how good it would be to have the same.

But I don't.

You can't choose your family.

HOME

Spring 2019, Zalaegerszeg

I have a lot of friends and with most of them, I can talk about everything. But real friends? Less than ten. With real friends, I don't need to use my head. These are friendships that have been formed decades ago. They're with kids I met at elementary school or boys I met when I came to Budapest.

Every visit to Zalaegerszeg is a trip back in time.

I stay in the house where I grew up. I stop by the pool and talk to János and Joe about the good old days, when our coach would spank us if we didn't pay attention to her orders.

I stop by Attila's bike shop and we talk about how we had to abandon my first Balaton swim because of the thunderstorm.

We laugh about it.

Time changes reality. All's well that ends well. What had once brought me to tears has become a funny tale to tell.

Those trips are a reminder of how far I've come. People greet me on the street. I don't always know who they are when I say hi to them, but it doesn't matter. They know me, they are happy to see me, they live in my hometown. That's all I need to know.

Things were simple when I was a kid. Things were good. Children don't play on the streets anymore. When I see them do so in old Hungarian movies, I travel back in time: This was my life and I wouldn't want to change it.

MY THIRD SECRET TO SUCCESS

Spring 2019, Hungary

I would be the worst swimmer in the world without a goal to work towards. But with a target, I can make myself fight and suffer endlessly in the pool. I just need to know why – and that goes down to the smallest level, to every move I am supposed to make. Over the years, I've had to do my fair share of less-than-fun training exercises, from kicking-only with small foot fins to the countless days spent with snorkels on my face.

I'm okay with all of that – but only if I know how it makes me a better swimmer. Take the small foot fins as an example. First, they work the abs. And second, because of the added resistance, the thighs need more oxygen, and that gets the rest of the body used to working with less. It's an added benefit that the extra-strong kicks become part of my muscle memory.

From the first day of my season, I know every meter I will have to swim. I get my training program from Nikos and he knows I will work my way through it without complaining. I'm old enough not to need somebody standing at the side of the pool, motivating me or correcting my form.

Training sessions can be long.

Very long.

Right now, it's seven hours per day.

When I'm in the water, I focus on the movements. The mind sometimes wanders, but the point of training is doing things the right way and I can't just rely on my muscle memory to take care of that.

When a physically intense workout lasts longer than two Lord of the Rings movies, it's better to only think of the exercise I'm currently doing rather than what's ahead. 4x20 laps are not scary. 4x120 laps can make you despair. Swimming 14 kilometers is exhausting enough by itself; I don't need my mind to mess with me.

I like to finish my trainings with paddles and a buoy. The body is like a turbo car – you can't just go full speed and then park it a second later. It's a good idea to slow down towards the end to get the recovery process started. When I can barely move after training, I'm happy. It means I did everything the right way.

NORTH CHANNEL III

August 2019, Northern Ireland

There is an old sign at Bangor's Eisenhower Pier. The rust growing on the iron nails in its corners has covered most of its turquoise metal, but the words are still legible.

"FROM HERE STARTED THE LONG HARD MARCH TO ALLIED VICTORY"
DWIGHT D. EISENHOWER

OPPOSITE THIS POINT WAS THE GATHERING AREA FOR A MASSIVE CONVOY OF MIXED SHIPS WHICH SAILED TO ARRIVE AT THE BEACHES OF NORMANDY ON D-DAY 6th. JUNE 1944.

In a few weeks, I will board the boat to the starting point on this pier.

I remember when I was reading the Wikipedia article on Folkestone, where I stayed before my English Channel swim. It said that the town was shelled by Nazi artillery.

Funny how things come full circle.

This time, I stay in Donaghadee so I don't need a rental car. I arrive on August 11, ten days before my window opens. The weather is outrageously bad, even for British "summer" standards. I keep the heating turned on for a whole week as the outside temperature doesn't even reach

15 degrees most days. Except for a morning swim and the daily swim with the Chunky Dunkers, I mostly keep to myself. It's such a great feeling to be back with the Dunkers after all that happened last year. "You're like a local to us," Martin, their leader, tells me. "They're all watching you swim like you're their son."

When I'm not swimming, my small room in walking distance to the sea is all I need. I relax, watch some TV shows and cook pasta. If I were to go meet the other channel swimmers, we would only talk about the swim. I've thought and talked about the North Channel more than enough. Now I'm in a good place and I intend to keep it that way, so I try to avoid the topic. All the extra planning discussions won't help me if the sea doesn't play along.

Every time I put on a new piece of clothing, I feel a weird scratch somewhere. When I find the source, it always is something beautiful. Móni and the girls have hidden lots of little letters and photos of the four of us in my luggage. Some envelopes have a date on it that tells me when I'm allowed to open it.

I may be on my own, but I'm not alone.

The days pass quickly. I don't spend much time consciously reflecting on the big picture. The thought that this is the final step to the peak is deeply ingrained in me, and that's all I need.

My window is open for seven days: August 21 to 27, Wednesday to Tuesday. On Wednesday, the weather starts to get better – not good enough for a swim yet, but at least I can spend some time outside without hating everything.

Padraig will be not only be my organizer again, this time he will also pilot the boat himself. After last year, my trust for him only has increased. He is a swimmer himself, so he knows what it takes. Padraig tells me that it looks like I'll swim on the weekend. That's perfectly fine with me. With every sunny day, the sea gets warmer. There are a few more people attempting the crossing, so even though Infinity has plenty of boats, the swimmers will be spread out on two days. I will be in the group that goes second.

I train, cook pasta, find letters from Móni and focus on myself. Despite everything that happened, I never worry. My insides feel like a perfectly still lake during a cold winter morning.

On Friday, I get confirmation: The first group will swim on Saturday, my group starts around dawn on Sunday.

I get up on Saturday to see the other swimmers off and get my body accustomed to waking up early. Since I arrived, I've never gone back to bed after waking up in the morning. It makes it easier to go to bed early that evening and the more my rhythm changes, the easier the swim will be.

Saturday is a calm day with beautiful weather. The TV crew comes over to do some filming, I relax, I instruct my crew on how I want the feedings to be done. It's the same plan as last year: a carb drink every 30 minutes, some candy every full hour.

Late that afternoon, the messages start coming in: Three of four swimmers finished! It turned out to be a perfect day for swimming, nice weather and a calm sea all the way to the Scottish coast.

As glad as I was in the morning not to be in the water, now I'm jealous of them.

I hear my alarm go off and I'm ready. 2 a.m., plenty of time to have breakfast, prepare my food, have coffee – and go to the toilet. I'd rather not start with a full stomach again.

I feel like a surgeon, doing one thing after another calmly and precisely.

Everything goes as planned and Martin from the Chunky Dunkers picks me up on time. We meet up with the others at the pier in Bangor and kill some time while the other boats get ready. There are four swimmers today, I will be the last one to start.

"It will be calm in the beginning, but a little rougher towards Scotland," Padraig tells me.

"Bring it on," I think.

Padraig is piloting the boat himself, Jacqui is with him. She doesn't seem to be feeling too well, but it feels great to have her with me. Yesterday, she sent me a lovely text wishing me good luck. She knew we wouldn't have much time to chat today.

We pack our stuff onto the boat and leave. A little tension cuts into my calmness, but I know that the odds are in my favor. It won't be fun, but I should make it to Scotland.

I've done the work. The kilometers in the pool, the hours in the gym, the nights spent working on my mind.

They put the anti-chafing, lanolin-based mixture called channel grease on me. I get ready. We get close to the Donaghadee lighthouse. I jump into the water. Without Ion, the send-off is a little less enthusiastic than last year.

Once I'm in the water, the calmness is back.

I'm here to do my job.

To the lighthouse, out of the water. The Chunky Dunkers are here again, cheering us on. I stand up and wave to the boat.

And then, I start my very last Oceans Seven swim.

Hopefully.

It's neither dark nor bright. A thick shroud of mist hides the sun and turns everything into a brown-greyish soup. As if a painter only had one color for the whole canvas, so he used a little more of it on the bottom, in this case the sea, and a little less above the waterline.

Good thing I'm not here to admire the landscape.

I feel strong. The water is about as cold as I expected it – or rather as "fresh", as Padraig likes to say. He has this amazing way of describing the water only as "fresh", "fresher", "very fresh" and "very f---ing fresh".

I make it to my first feeding without any incidents. No jellyfish, no significant waves, no unexpected currents.

The same goes for the second feeding.

After an hour, the mist slowly clears.

I swim. Time passes. I swim. Nothing bad happens.

By the time I get my sixth snack, the sun is shining on me and inside me. That's three hours without anything bad happening.

I have made a pact with Padraig: For the first six hours, I will swim at a pace that I'd consider relaxed. Then, I can go all out. Padraig wanted to make sure that I don't risk finishing for the sake of any time records, and he has my full trust, so I gave him my word.

I swim below my limit and fate rewards me with beautiful conditions. A flat sea, a sunny sky, and probably some dolphins. I can't see them myself, but everybody on the boat gathers on one side and looks at the water ahead of me. I'm just glad I don't have to worry about them having spotted a shark, so I keep swimming.

It feels so easy. The cold doesn't get to me at all and I've only been slightly grazed by jellyfish twice. Just the devil walking by and whispering: "I'm still here, but I've hurt you enough last year".

After the sixth hour, the sea gets a little choppier. I don't care, Padraig had warned me before the start.

Does the final act need to be harder? I don't care. Maybe this is the reward for everything I've gone through. A joy swim to finish it all off.

Stroke, stroke, kick.

Time passes. A wave hits me.

Stroke, stroke, kick.

At times, I hear a faint whistling: Watch out, a jellyfish. The whistling comes from a spotter on the boat, telling me that I need to pay attention to him as he'll either wave me towards or away from the boat to avoid swimming into a jellyfish. If a sound much sharper than the ordinary whistling cuts through the air like a blade, I know it is urgent: Padraig has gotten involved, whistling with two fingers in his mouth. The noise he generates this way is unreal.

Now that I must be far past the halfway mark, I hear his whistles a lot more often. It's not always a lion's mane jellyfish, but I still make sure to follow the directions I'm given – and it helps. I avoid the worst.

Feedings are starting to feel like much-needed breaks.

It's hard to explain how grueling swimming becomes after eight hours. Imagine swimming at a fast pace in a pool for four lanes. Imagine how your arms feel: the burn, the exhaustion.

Now imagine doing this for two hours. You can watch a full-length movie at the cinema in that time, but imagine you're swimming instead. No breaks. Imagine the tide dragging you sideways with every stroke. Imagine you keep swimming for, let's say, the duration of a 200-kilometer car ride on the highway. Now imagine high waves crashing into you from every direction, imagine how every third breath is full of water. Then, imagine you stay in the water for as long as a typical three-course family dinner would take. And then, you watch an entire football match on TV. Swimming.

So that's two hours at the movies, a long drive to see your relatives, a drawn-out dinner with them, and a game of football. Does that sound like a long day? Try it swimming at the fast pace you normally do at the pool, but with the waves crashing down on you and the bitterly cold water numbing your limbs.

This is what I'm doing today.

Another hour passes. The waves are getting higher and I feel the current pushing me away.

As I prepare to swim away from the boat after a feeding, I make a mistake. I tilt my head up and look towards Scotland. It's exactly where it was 30 minutes ago.

For the next few minutes, I don't feel like I'm moving forward.

For the third time, a massive rogue wave carries me a few meters to the side. At least the boat is so small that it's being carried towards me a little by the waves, so I don't have to put too much effort in getting back to it.

Swim. Swim. Swim. My arms burn as they did before, but I'm not getting rewarded for it anymore. Every feeding is a painful reminder: If what the guys on the boat tell me is correct, I've only swam two kilometers in the last two hours.

The ocean can be a bottomless pit of cruelty.

Swim.

The cold is grabbing my insides. I can feel its unstoppable, icy hands moving through my skin, slowly cutting through all that precious brown fat I have built. In my mind, I can almost see the faint blue trace the hands leave behind.

Yet, I move my arms forward. Pull them back strongly. Drag them out of the water. Lunge forward again. Tens of thousands of times.

Push it.

My ten-hour feeding. "Three kilometers to go," they shout from the boat.

I feel broken.

Well, considering I've been in here for ten hours, I feel okay. I just can't seem to make progress.

It's gotten a little better since those terrible two hours. I passed the point where the current was the strongest, but I'm still far from moving fast. I've swum with the same power, the same stroke rate, the same fire all day. Yet, if you were to chart my pace, the line would look like a damn rollercoaster.

Swim. The cold's icy fingers keep reaching into my chest. Swim.

Ten hours and 30 minutes: another feeding. A warm drink. I ask for some extra candy. In my three tries crossing the North Channel, I've never done that. But I need all the energy I can get.

On I go. In the distance, I can see a rocky, green-brown slope. Scotland is getting closer. The sun is out. Even the waves are getting smaller.

Swim.

Eleven hours: feeding time. As I'm drinking, Jacqui shows up and says something. I can only understand "kilometers" through my earplugs. "Huh?" I ask, shaking my head.

"Two k!", she says.

"Ooooh my god." That's the only response I can muster.

They cheer me on as I start swimming again. With these currents, swimming two kilometers feels like crossing an entire ocean. The current usually gets weaker towards the coast here, but I'm exhausted.

Hopefully, this was my last feeding. If I make progress, they will surely skip the one that would come in half an hour. I have about seventy minutes to beat the overall record.

In the pool, it would take me 29 minutes to finish.

Here, I have no clue if I can do it. Only one way to find out.

Swim.

The maddening thing about swimming in the ocean is that it becomes impossible to estimate distances. When I look up, Scotland is...well, there. When I look up again later, it may have moved, but I have no idea how much closer I've gotten or how far away it is.

I'll know once I'm on the beach.

I've always taken pride in finishing without having any energy left. When I felt too good after the finish in Gibraltar, I was angry. For a while, I was worried that it would be like this again today – after all, I had promised Padraig not to push it for six hours.

So much for arriving with too much left in my tank. It's almost empty.

Every stroke feels like somebody has put shards of broken glass into my shoulders. My arms are confused whether they are freezing or burning.

Swim. To swim is the solution.

I grind the glass shards in my joints and muscles to dust, only for them to be replaced by iron nails. I pulverize those into nothing, only for drops of molten lava to take their place.

"Pain is temporary," I've said in better, drier, less exhausting times.

"Úszás!", I tell myself now, "Swim!"

I speed up. Stroke by stroke, kick by kick, I get closer to Scotland.

If my head were clearer, I'd be surprised at the pace I'm going. But all I'm doing now is swim.

It must have been about an hour since my last feeding. My best guess would be that the coast is 500 meters away, but what do I know. I'm just here to swim.

Swim.

The boat has stopped.

I realize this and stop swimming to look in front of me. Scotland is right there. There are fewer waves and the current is gone.

Ahead of me and a bit to the right, there are some rocks. They would count as a finish point. Padraig told me to just touch them and come back.

Further ahead to my left is the beach, inviting me to walk out just like I walked into the English Channel. I began this journey six years ago, almost to the day.

I think of John Maclean and how he pulled himself onto the dry sand. That old documentary that got me into solo swims hadn't crossed my mind in months, but now it's like I just saw it yesterday. I see Maclean going the extra mile, dragging his legs for those last few meters before celebrating. I remember how I felt cheering in front of the TV, how I waited for years so I could swim with the same boat.

I slightly turn to the left. If I miss the record by a few minutes, so be it. When I started this, I did it for my happiness, not any numbers.

As I pass the rocks heading towards the beach, I enter heaven.

Push.

It.

I push with every fiber in my body, with every feeling in my soul, with every thought in my brain. With me are all the people I love, all my supporters, everybody who walked with me on this journey.

I swim in perfect form. I breathe properly.

Scotland must be a beautiful country.

The thought of slowing down tries to enter my head and I kick it straight back out all the way to the coast. I pull my arms a little harder, tense my core a little more to float perfectly.

I see the sand below me.

The last strokes of my Oceans Seven journey.

The water is shallow. I stand up.

I explode in emotion. I am in pure bliss; the greatest moment I could ever have.

I walk out with heavy legs. My knees appear from the water. I never have to swim in this cold water again.

I keep going until I'm all the way out and turn around. I raise my arms. Victory.

I hear screams from the boat.

I made it.

For a few precious moments, my mind is empty, yet full.

I remember the time I needed for the overall world record. It must have been a matter of minutes, which feels a little ridiculous considering the record stands around 64 hours.

I want to know.

The boat is far away. Turns out I will have to get back in the water, but so be it. The swim back passes in what feels like seconds.

Pain and pride, daze and delight. Bedlam and bliss.

I fight my way up the three steps of the boat's ladder.

Now, I can share the victory. I start crying.

Jacqui hugs me.

I hear the word: record.

"Four minutes! You made it by four minutes," someone screams at me.

I hug Padraig.

There are no words to describe this feeling, so this is where my story ends.

My last Oceans Seven swim started with British weather…

…but I got to finish in beautiful conditions.

I will always be thankful to Dr. Bob Darling (above) and the whole Ulster hospital staff, among them Dave and Julie (below). Without them, I wouldn't be here today.

EPILOGUE

August 2021

A lot has happened since the day I finished my Oceans Seven journey. Well, a lot, but also nothing at the same time. Since the beginning of the Covid-19 pandemic, almost all competitions have been cancelled. I was lucky to have the capability to train in my backyard: In a small pool, I've got a machine that creates an artificial current I can swim against. It's like a treadmill, but for swimmers. Taking care of the twins during home-schooling showed me that swimming may not be the most exhausting thing in the world after all.

As a pulmonary infection became the dominating topic of discussion around the world, I decided to pay my asthma doctor a long-overdue visit. After she had me do some tests, she looked at me like a concerned parent. "You have a lung capacity of 62 percent," she said before scolding me for not using my inhalator in the past two decades. I never felt like I needed that extra help, but I decided that from now on, I will use it regularly.

Knowing how weak my lungs were during my Oceans Seven swims fills me with an extra ounce of pride. To me, it proves that succeeding in this sport is not about talent or physical gift, but only about willpower and how much you really want it.

The summer of 2021 marked the start of my next big journey: the Stillwater Eight. It is a series proposed by Michelle Macy, an open water legend and the third person to ever finish the Oceans Seven. The Stillwater Eight includes stretches of Lake Ontario in Canada, Lake Tahoe in the US, Lake Taupo in New Zealand, Lake Zürich in Switzerland, Loch Ness in Scotland, Lake Malawi in Malawi, the Sea of Galilee in Israel, and Lake Titicaca in Bolivia. Each of the swims comes with its own challenges, from the freezing waters of Loch Ness to Lake Titicaca's location at a challenging altitude of 3,812 meters above sea level.

As a warm-up for Lake Zürich, I competed at a race in Hallstatt, Austria. We arrived late on the night before the swim and in the morning, I had to drive around the lake after missing the boat to the starting point. I felt terrible throughout the race. Having only a week to regroup and get ready for Zürich, I was worried that I would fail my first attempt.

I shouldn't have worried. The organizers, my pilot and my feeding helper were perfectly reliable and I didn't feel at all like the week before. Due to the many training kilometers I had missed out on, I was still slower than I used to be. I had to let many swimmers pass me in the beginning, but I felt good despite the chilly 17-degree Celsius water. About halfway through the course, it rained heavily for about 45 minutes. Visibility was close to zero and when the rain stopped, I saw someone frantically scooping water out of the boat with a bucket. To my surprise, Móni was waiting at the finish in Zürich, grinning from ear to ear. "You finished first!" she told me. I must have passed the others in the rain, I just didn't see them. Because I wasn't at my physical best, I didn't feel the same pride I normally would after an Ocean swim, but 26 kilometers in nine hours and 17 minutes – and a race win – is good enough.

Most importantly, I have a mission again. Nothing may ever come close to finishing the Oceans Seven, but I am excited for what's ahead.

MY OCEANS SEVEN IN NUMBERS

ENGLISH CHANNEL
August 20, 2013 – 10 hours, 47 minutes – 47.23 kilometers

TSUGARU STRAIT
August 9, 2014 – 7 hours, 29 minutes – 30 kilometers

MOLOKA'I CHANNEL
September 22 to 23, 2015 – 12 hours, 2 minutes – 54 kilometers

CATALINA CHANNEL
October 5, 2015 – 10 hours, 59 minutes – 34 kilometers

COOK STRAIT
April 22, 2017 – 6 hours, 57 minutes, 49 seconds – 30 kilometers

STRAIT OF GIBRALTAR
November 2, 2017 – 4 hours, 9 minutes – 15.2 kilometers

NORTH CHANNEL
August 26, 2019 – 12 hours, 11 minutes, 20 seconds – 40 kilometers

ABOUT THE AUTHORS

Attila Mányoki is one of the most successful marathon swimmers in the world. You can find him at @attilamanyoki on Instagram. As of August 2021, he still holds the world records for the fastest overall Oceans Seven time and for the fastest crossing of the Kaiwi Channel.

Martin Schauhuber is an award-winning sportswriter and podcast host for the Austrian newspaper Der Standard. You can find him at @Mar_Schau on Twitter. As of August 2021, he is not holding any world records.

Printed in Great Britain
by Amazon